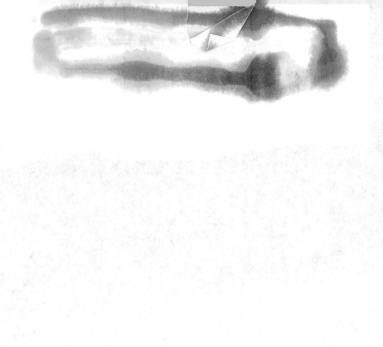

Kindly Keep It Covered

A comedy

Dave Freeman

Samuel French — London
New York - Toronto - Hollywood

© 1997 BY DAVE FREEMAN

KINDLY KEEP IT COVERED

First presented by Bill Kenwright in association with the
Churchill Theatre, Bromley on 9th March 1988, at the
Churchill Theatre, with the following cast of characters:

Roland Dickerby	Terry Scott
Julia Dickerby	Amanda Barrie
Olivia	Andrée Melly
Sidney	Robin Nedwell
Vanessa	Anita Graham
Hooper	Chris Sanders
Campbell	John Pennington

Directed by Martin Connor
Designed by Colin Winslow

CHARACTERS

Roland Dickerby
Julia Dickerby
Olivia
Sidney
Vanessa
Hooper
Woman Police Sergeant Campbell

SYNOPSIS OF SCENES

The action takes place in the reception area of a country health spa

Act I   Midsummer's Eve. 8 p.m.
Act II   Ten minutes later

Time—the present

Other plays by Dave Freeman,
published by Samuel French Ltd

A Bedfull of Foreigners
Key for Two (*with John Chapman*)

ACT I

The reception lounge of a health spa, which was formally an old country house. Midsummer's Eve. 8 p.m.

UC is an archway which leads to an enclosed terrace, running left to right. L it leads to the gardens. R it leads to the sauna and plunge pool. The back wall of the terrace is glassed in and the grounds are just visible behind it. UL, set in a small alcove is a reception desk with a key-board behind it. DL from this is a cupboard with a pair of narrow louvred doors. Further DL is an archway which leads to the rest of the building, the treatment room and the back door to the gardens. URC is a fancy fountain-type water dispenser with a tap, and paper cup container. A sign over the tap reads "Cliffbank Magna Waters, drink freely". UR is a large old-fashioned open fireplace. DR of this is a small narrow chest of drawers. Further DR is a door marked "Office". There is a three-seater sofa and a large Windsor armchair. Concealed behind a screen, on a trolley, is a life-sized dummy dressed as a waiter wearing a fez

When the CURTAIN rises, the stage is empty

Roland appears in the centre archway. He is in early middle age and permanently harassed. He doubles into view and then does an about turn still doubling. He addresses an invisible group of joggers, holding himself erect like a PT Instructor

Roland One two, one two, halt. Thank you, everybody, that was splendid. The next jogging session eight o'clock in the morning. See you then. (*He remains for a moment and then staggers towards the desk where he collapses, utterly exhausted, as he gains his breath*)

Hooper enters UC. He is a very stout man, even more exhausted than Roland. He staggers up behind Roland and stops, panting for breath

Roland doesn't see him. The pair of them crawl forward hand over hand along the desk until Hooper puts his hand out and clutches Roland's shoulder. Roland gives a cry of surprise and turns to see him, and then with a supreme effort pulls himself together and adopts a cheery manner

(*Brightly*) Ah, Mr Hooper.

Hooper (*groaning*) Uuuhh.

Roland The jog is over. You're finished.

Hooper Oh, I'm finished all right. I'm bloody dying.

Roland No you're not.

Hooper Dickerby, I'm on my last legs. Oh my God, I must be mad, what am I doing here?

Roland You're getting fit and losing weight. (*He picks up a clipboard*) Do you realize that since you've been here you've lost seven pounds?

Hooper Well I'd like it back.

Roland Mr Hooper, there's no gain without pain. Don't you want to be fit?

Hooper I *was* fit until I came here.

Roland (*losing his patience*) Look, what have you followed me in here for?

Hooper I want some food, Dickerby. I must have some food and I want it now. I can't wait until supper.

Roland There is no supper tonight.

Hooper is so shocked he nearly falls over. He clasps at Roland, who is also a trifle unsteady and they rock around together, until Roland steadies himself

Hooper What do you mean, no supper?

Roland If you listened and read the notices you'd know that tonight we are holding a Midsummer's Night Dance.

Hooper Dance? I can't dance. I can't even stand up. I want food. I want supper.

Roland Well, instead of supper we have a special buffet laid on at the dance. You can go over there and help yourself.

Hooper You mean we can have as much as we like?

Roland Within reason.

Hooper Is it proper food?

Roland Of course it's proper food. Go over and see for yourself. It's in the gymnasium. Now if you don't mind I'm busy.

Hooper All right, but before I go I think there is something you ought to know. You being so strict on our diets.

Roland Yes?

Hooper The man in the next chalet to me has a big tin of biscuits.

Roland Biscuits?

Hooper Chocolate biscuits.

Roland Oh that's disgraceful.

Hooper Isn't it? And what's more the mean bastard won't give me one.

Hooper staggers towards the centre archway and exits to the gardens

Roland staggers to the sofa and lays sprawled out on it

Julia enters. A nice natured, attractive girl

Julia Are you all right, darling?
Roland Yes, just worn out.
Julia Oh poor darling.

Roland sits up and she sits on the sofa beside him and cradles his head on her shoulders

Roland I'm not cut out for this life, Julia, all this health food and exercise. It's undermining my system.
Julia It's not, darling. You look so much better than when we bought the place.
Roland Do I?
Julia Oh you do.
Roland I don't feel better.
Julia That's because you don't remember how unfit you were before.
Roland Oh great, I've not only got sore feet and a bad back, I'm losing my memory.
Julia You've just had a rotten day.
Roland Oh I have yes. I can remember that.
Julia All that bother at the auction sale, when you bid for the wrong lot.
Roland It wasn't my fault.
Julia Oh I'm not blaming you, darling. Only I'd rather Mummy didn't find out.
Roland I don't care if she finds out or not. I am not intimidated by your mother, Julia.
Julia I know you're not, darling.

Julia gets up, goes to the screen and folds it back revealing a life size dummy dressed as a waiter wearing a fez. Around its neck is a large menu card which reads: The Ali Baba Café menu
                              Shish kebab
                              Steak and bacon pudding
                              Jam roly poly
                              Spotted dick

It's just that I'd sooner avoid trouble if we can. Where is the Ali Baba Café?
Roland In receivership. The auction was full of their stuff. (*After a short pause*) What have you done with the stuffed camel?
Julia I had the men put it in the sauna out of the way. I don't want Mummy seeing it.
Roland No, perhaps you're right.

Julia What will you do with it?

Roland Oh I'll put it back in the next auction ...

Julia It's a stuffed camel, Roland, supposing nobody buys it?

Roland Oh, some idiot will buy it. I mean I did.

Julia Yes, still if Mummy ever sees it she'll say you'd been drinking.

Roland Of course I hadn't. I had half a pint of lager with my lunch. I walked into that auction sale stone cold sober and look what we got. *Him* and a stuffed camel. Imagine what I'd have bought if I'd been drunk.

Olivia enters from the gardens. She is a smartly dressed lady in middle age, with an air of authority. She stops at the entrance

Olivia Oh good-evening, sir, are you being attended to?

Roland If you're talking to *him*, Olivia, you'll wait a long time for an answer.

Olivia (*walking forward*) Oh, it's a dummy.

Roland Yes.

Olivia What on earth is it doing here?

Roland (*defiantly*) I bought it in the auction.

Olivia Why?

Julia flashes a glance at Roland

Roland Well, I er — bought some bed linen, and they threw that in.

Olivia Threw it in?

Roland Yes.

Olivia I wasn't born yesterday, Roland, you bought that thing by mistake. You bid for the wrong lot.

Roland Oh no I didn't.

Olivia I suppose you had been drinking.

Roland Certainly not.

Olivia I don't mind you drinking in moderation.

Roland That's most kind of you.

Olivia But when you get so befuddled you buy rubbish.

Roland Olivia, I have not been drinking.

Olivia Roland, I can smell your breath.

Roland No you can't.

Olivia Oh yes I can — and you reek of peppermint. It reminds me of Julia's first husband.

Julia Look, if you're going to bring him up, I'm leaving.

Julia exits to the gardens

Roland I don't know why you had to mention Sidney. You know how it upsets her.

Olivia I can't see why, I mean you both did very well out of him.

Roland (*stung*) What do you mean by that?

Olivia Well, for start *you* were the insurance man who sold him the policy.

Roland So what?

Olivia With a double indemnity if he should die in an accident.

Roland It was a tragedy, Olivia, a terrible tragedy.

Olivia Not that much of a tragedy

Roland No, not for you, no. You were his mother-in-law. But it was for my insurance company. He'd only paid one premium.

Olivia They never recovered his body.

Roland That's hardly surprising. He drove off the edge of a quarry on to a hut full of dynamite. But we still paid up.

Olivia Yes, in the end.

Roland Due on no small part to the battle I fought on Julia's behalf.

Olivia Yes, you saw that she got the money.

Roland I did yes.

Olivia And then you married her.

Roland And what's wrong with that? We fell in love.

Olivia (*coldly*) Yes. Now what about this dummy. We can't leave it here.

Roland I wasn't going to.

Olivia Look at that menu around its neck. We're supposed to be running a *health farm*.

Olivia lifts the menu off the dummy

Roland wheels the dummy off to the office, puts it inside and then returns

(*Reading the menu*) Shish kebab, bacon pudding. Roly poly pudding. Sheer unadulterated poison. (*Horrified*) Spotted *dick!*

Roland Yes. Spotted dick.

Olivia How disgusting. The very acme of trash food. (*She puts the menu down*)

The telephone rings and Roland goes into the office L *to answer it, closing the door behind him*

Julia enters

Julia The band's turned up.

Olivia Oh good, I was worried about them. They weren't sure if they could make it.

Julia Who did you book in the end?

Olivia A jazz band called the Swinging Truncheons.

Julia The Swinging Truncheons?

Olivia Yes, dear, they're four policemen who raise money for charity.

Julia Oh well, why not? I suppose it keeps them off the streets.

Olivia To be perfectly honest, you get a much better class of jazz musician in the police force. You don't get them bringing those funny cigarettes along.

Julia Are they any good?

Olivia I've no idea, but it's only jazz, so I don't suppose it matters.

Roland comes in from the office

Roland A man just rang up about the chef's job.

Julia Was his name McTavish?

Roland Yes.

Olivia Oh good. What did he sound like?

Julia Very eccentric.

Roland Yes, isn't he?

Olivia You can't tell that over the phone, you should have let me speak to him.

Roland Well he's ringing back later — when he gets loose.

Olivia What do you mean gets loose?

Roland According to him, he's being held prisoner on a flying saucer by aliens. He's cooking them sausages, egg and chips.

Olivia Rubbish.

Roland I suppose it is, but they can eat what they like, they're aliens.

Roland goes back into the office and shuts the door

Olivia There are times when I think he's worse than Sidney.

Julia Well you hated the sight of him.

Olivia That's not true. I didn't dislike Sidney that much. It's true he was a thief, and a cheat and a liar and on top of that he had some very irritating habits.

Julia I know all about his habits.

Julia exits DL

Olivia goes and picks up the menu card

Olivia Especially that dreadful way he blew his nose. It sounded like a stampeding elephant. I can still hear it.

Off, Sidney is heard blowing his nose loudly

Olivia stops and freezes. Then the fountain makes a series of equally loud gurgling noises and she breathes a sigh of relief

Oh it's the fountain. We must get that seen to.

Olivia exits DL *as Sidney enters from the gardens. He is a suave rogue with a charming manner. He wears sunglasses and is dressed in a lightweight tropical suit and hat. He blows his nose loudly once more on a large red bandanna handkerchief, and then puts it away. He looks around him and goes to the counter as Vanessa Harbinger enters from the gardens. She is in early middle age, pleasant and slightly gullible. She is carrying a suitcase*

Vanessa Oh good-evening, I've just arrived.

Sidney answers her in a French accent. He is obviously quite ready to make a conquest. Throughout the play, it will become evident that Sidney speaks in a French accent when Vanessa, Hooper or Sergeant Campbell are present but in his own voice at other times

Sidney And so have I, madame.
Vanessa Is there anybody about?
Sidney Apparently not — just the two of us.
Vanessa Well there seems to be some sort of function going on in the other building.
Sidney Yes, I heard the music.
Vanessa Perhaps they're all over there.
Sidney Yes, so why don't we go over together and look?

He takes her arm. Vanessa though quite taken with him, is a little nervous, and she lightly disengages herself

Vanessa Why don't you go? And I'll wait here.
Sidney As you wish, madame, you are so enchanting I hope we shall meet again later.
Vanessa (*vaguely*) Yes.

Sidney crosses to the centre archway, turns, raises his hat, bows and exits to the gardens

Vanessa, obviously impressed, pats her hair

Olivia enters DL

Olivia Good-evening.

Vanessa Oh good-evening, My name is Harbinger, I believe you are expecting us. We're booked in for a fortnight.

Olivia Oh, Mrs Harbinger — of course, yes. How do you do. I'm Olivia de Vere.

Vanessa Then you must be Roland's mother-in-law.

Olivia Yes.

Vanessa How nice for you.

Olivia (*after a pause*) How well do you know Roland?

Vanessa Oh, we've never met.

Olivia I thought not.

Vanessa No, but my husband speaks of him quite often. They were colleagues when Roland worked for the Kindly Mutual Insurance Company.

Olivia Oh I *see*. Is your husband with you?

Vanessa He was held up. He's catching a train down later.

Olivia Well, I'm sure he and Roland will have lots to talk about. In the meantime perhaps you'd like to unpack.

They are at the desk now

Here we are. Chalet nine. We'll wait until you're both here before we process you in.

Vanessa And what does that entail?

Olivia Oh, just checking your weight and health. Then we decide what regime to put you on.

Vanessa Well it's more for Henry than me. He's put so much weight on lately.

Olivia I'm sure we'll soon have that off him. I'll take you to your chalet. (*She picks up the suitcase*) Oh it's quite heavy. Did you bring any food with you?

Vanessa No. I thought it was provided.

Olivia It is, but some people try to bring in extra.

Vanessa Really?

Olivia Yes, chocolate fudge, doughnuts, cream cakes — completely defeats the object of coming here.

Olivia and Vanessa exit to the gardens as Roland enters from the office. He picks up the guest register and is looking at it as Hooper moves silently in from DL *and comes up behind him. Hooper taps him on the shoulder and Roland starts*

Roland Mr Hooper, will you stop following me around. What do you want?

Hooper Food.

Roland Then I've told you. Go to the buffet in the gymnasium.

Hooper I've been there, Dickerby. All they've got are sticks of celery and bits of carrot. I'm not a bloody rabbit. I want proper food. You've got some proper food hidden away here somewhere. I know you have.

Roland No we haven't. All we have here is a vegetarian, low calorie, low salt, low fat, high fibre diet.

Hooper Yes, that's for my lot. What about the other lot?

Roland What other lot?

Hooper There's two sorts of food here. Two separate menus. One for us and one for *them*.

Roland I don't know what you mean by *them*. Who are they?

Hooper I don't know who they are. But I know what they eat. (*From behind his back he produces the cardboard menu which the dummy was holding*) Shish kebab, bacon pudding, jam roly poly and spotted dick. Look at it and then tell me who's on this diet. Who are they?

Roland Nobody.

Hooper Come on, Dickerby, who are they?

Roland Nobody, it's just an old piece of cardboard. Give it to me and I'll burn it.

Hooper No. I don't believe you. There's some sort of secret society around here that eats suet pudding — and I'm going to find it and join 'em.

Roland Well good luck.

Hooper exits DL *as Olivia enters from the gardens. She is carrying a large plastic bag. She holds it up*

Olivia Look at this.

Roland What is it?

Olivia Mrs Pinkerton just gave it to me. It's her husband.

Roland He must have shrunk a bit. What happened to him?

Olivia takes out a large tin of chocolate biscuits from the bag

Olivia He had this tin of chocolate biscuits hidden under the bed. Luckily she found it hidden and confiscated it.

Roland Oh, I was told about those.

Olivia And you took no action.

Roland I haven't had a chance, I've been busy all day.

Olivia Yes, down the pub.

Roland (*going to take them*) Give them to me, I'll put them somewhere safe.

Olivia Oh no, you can't be trusted with these, Roland. You're a chocoholic. Or worse an alcoholic chocoholic.

Roland Rubbish.

He goes to take them, Olivia holds them over her head

Olivia You've no will power, Roland; alcohol, chocolate, you'll weaken.
Roland Don't be ridiculous. Give me the biscuits.
Olivia No.
Roland Olivia, I've reformed. I haven't touched chocolate since I was at the
    Kindly Mutual. And ate half a chocolate cake.
Olivia Who ate the other half, Harry Harbinger?
Roland How did you know?
Olivia His wife just told me.
Roland Mrs Harbinger?
Olivia Yes they've just booked in for a fortnight.
Roland Oh good. I sent them a brochure.
Olivia It doesn't embarrass you having him here? Someone from the Kindly
    Mutual.
Roland Why should it? They don't hold grudges. Sidney was insured with
    them. He dies and they paid out. Had they found anything in the least bit
    suspicious I can assure you, Henry Harbinger would not be coming to stay
    here, reduced rates or not.
Olivia What reduced rates?
Roland The ones I mentioned when I sent him the brochure.
Olivia Well thank you for informing me. There could have been a very nasty
    scene when they came to settle the bill.
Roland I see, so that's all the thanks I get for drumming up business.

Roland stalks off DL. *Olivia goes to the cupboard and puts the shopping bag
inside, then exits* DL

Hooper enters from the gardens

*He looks around. He is searching for food. He opens the drawers in the chest
of drawers and the goes to the cupboard, he rummages around and finds the
chocolate biscuits. Then we hear Sidney blowing his nose off stage*

Hooper goes into the cupboard and pulls the door shut

Sidney enters from the garden and looks around

*Hooper in the cupboard coughs as he chokes on a biscuit. Sidney goes to the
cupboard and listens. Then he opens the door*

Hooper steps out eating a biscuit

Sidney (*with the assumed French accent*) Are you all right?
Hooper Yes, fine — just checking the bed biscuits.
Sidney The what?

Hooper The linen beds — bed bugs — bed linen. Are you staying here?
Sidney No, I have just arrived. My word it gets quite chilly here in England. I think I have caught a cold. (*He pulls his handkerchief out. Caught in its folds is a passport which falls to the floor unnoticed by him. He blows his nose and puts the handkerchief back in his pocket*)
Hooper Well it's bound to be a bit nippy, it's midsummer's night. Where have you come from?
Sidney Madagascar. You know where that is?
Hooper Yes, it's a big island off the coast of Africa, isn't it?
Sidney *Mais oui.* Very big, very warm. Not like here.
Hooper Are you a Madagascarite, or whatever they call them?
Sidney A Malagasy? No, I am a citizen of France. My name is Doctor Louis la Roullière. (*He pats his pocket*) I have my passport here somewhere. Don't tell me I have lost it.

Sidney continues to pat his pockets. Hooper spots the passport on the floor and picks it up unseen by Sidney who finds second passport in his jacket. Hooper takes a quick glance inside passport

Sidney ⎫
Hooper ⎭ (*together*) Here it is.

Sidney gives a jolly, long laugh

Sidney Ahah, you have found my other passport.
Hooper Yes.
Sidney Yes, I always carry a spare one.
Hooper Why is that?
Sidney In case I lose one.
Hooper You said you were a doctor.
Sidney Doctor Louis la Roullière. *Voilà.*

Sidney opens up the second passport and shows it, and tries to take the first passport from Hooper. But Hooper has already looked in it. He looks again

Hooper This one says you're Polish. Pan Stanislaus — prizh — priszhk. Pzik.
Sidney Please don't try and pronounce it. You will only hurt yourself.

Sidney takes the passport away from Hooper. Sidney now adopts a mysterious air. A character from a spy drama

Obviously I now have to tell you the truth. Have you heard of the *Deuxième Bureau*, the French secret service?

Hooper Is that who you are?

Sidney *Oui*, but nobody must know. Had you not seen my other passport, I would not have mentioned it.

Hooper Have the *Deuxième* Thingummy sent you here to lose weight?

Sidney Ah *non*, I am not fat like you. I have come here to find a woman.

Hooper Find a woman?

Sidney *Oui*.

Hooper Well you're in luck. There's no shortage of *women* here. It's food we're short of.

Sidney Ah no. I am looking for one *particular* woman. She go by the name Madame Dickerby.

Hooper Oh she runs the place with her husband. Roland Dickerby.

Sidney Ah Roland Dickerby. I will see him first. Could you find him for me and bring him here?

Hooper What's it about? Is he in trouble?

Sidney Ah *non*.

Hooper Oh what a pity.

Sidney It's just we think he can help us with our enquiries. Is there somewhere round here I could see him on his own?

Hooper Try the office.

Sidney Good, I shall wait for him there. Oh just tell him an old friend wish to see him.

Sidney goes into the office and closes the door

Hooper waits until he has gone and then makes a bee line for the cupboard. He opens the cupboard door and is about to go inside

Roland enters from DL

Roland What are you doing?

Hooper Nothing. Just checking.

Roland Checking what?

Hooper Well, you see there's an old friend waiting to see you.

Roland Well where is he?

Hooper He's hiding?

Roland peers into the cupboard

Roland I can't see him.

Hooper Not in here. Over there in the office.

Roland Are you feeling all right?

Hooper No, I feel dreadful. I want some food. Proper food.

Roland Now come on, Mr Hooper, use some will power. Go back to the buffet, fill up on celery and tell yourself you mean to stick it.

Hooper And that's what you can do with your celery, Dickerby. Stick it.

Hooper exits to the gardens. Roland goes to the office, opens the door and enters. After a second, he staggers out again in a state of semi collapse

Roland Oh my God. Oh no.

Sidney comes out of the office. He is now using his normal voice

Get away from me. Whatever you are and wherever you came from, keep away. (*He picks up two pencils and holds them like a crucifix*) Keep away, keep away.

Sidney That's for vampires, Roland. I'm not a vampire, I'm not even a ghost.

Roland I've only your word for that. You could be anything.

Sidney I'm alive, Roland. Now stop flapping about like a wet hen and put away your pencils.

Roland Oh my God. I need a drink.

Sidney I'll have one with you.

Roland No you won't. We haven't got any. We're teetotal. Well you must be real. I mean you're not a hallucination are you?

Sidney Most certainly not. No, I'm quite real. I mean you can pinch me.

Roland If you're alive, Sidney, it'll be Scotland Yard who'll pinch you.

Sidney Then let's say I am officially dead, and that's the way I want to keep it.

Roland You've given me a dreadful shock, Sidney. What happened to you?

Sidney (*warily*) Well, what did you hear?

Roland Well you were on the Continent selling dodgy antiques when, according to Julia, all hell broke loose. The Inland Revenue wanted you for tax evasion.

Sidney That's possible.

Roland Then the V.A.T. lot came into it and finally the police issued a warrant for your arrest. Poor Julia was frantic.

Sidney Yes, I suppose she was, poor girl.

Roland The next thing we heard was your van had driven off the edge of a quarry and landed on a hut full of explosives. There was nothing left.

Sidney Nothing?

Roland Well almost nothing. They found one of your shoes, a number plate and the leg off a fake Chippendale cabinet.

Sidney (*pained*) Not *fake*, Roland. Restored.

Roland Oh, restored.

Sidney Restored to its original condition.

Roland Like you.

Sidney How nicely put.

Roland So what happened?

Sidney Well as you gathered, it wasn't me in the van.

Roland Then who was it?

Sidney Well it was some tatty villain who had mugged me.

Roland Mugged you?

Sidney Yes. I'd given him a lift, and he banged me over the head, pushed me out of the van and drove off with everything I had. I tried to get a lift to go after him when three police cars went screaming past. I think they must have been after me.

Roland Only they went after him instead.

Sidney Exactly. He put his foot down hard, skidded round a bend. The next thing I heard was the explosion.

Roland Dreadful.

Sidney (*cheerfully*) Yes wasn't it. Anyway the next morning there was a picture of me all over the newspapers with the headline, Foreign Criminal Dies in Police Chase. I thought that was a bit much, calling me foreign.

Roland But you didn't complain to them.

Sidney No, I lay low for a bit — then got a job on a tramp steamer and went to Madagascar.

Roland Then why have you come back now?

Sidney Well, now I've been officially declared dead, Julia should have been given the key to my safe deposit.

Roland Yes, there was nothing in it. Just a box with a few odds and ends.

Sidney And a key?

Roland Er yes, I believe there was a key — yes.

Sidney A key to another safe deposit box.

Roland Yes, but we could never find out where it was.

Sidney *You* weren't meant to.

Roland Well not *me* specifically. I meant Julia. She was your widow.

Sidney Until you married her.

Roland (*worried*) Oh you heard about that?

Sidney Yes.

There is a pause, then suddenly Sidney plunges his hand into his inside pocket. Roland panics and puts his hands up. Sidney pulls out a large cigar

Congratulations, have a cigar.

Roland Well that's awfully nice of you — but now you're back.

Sidney Oh don't worry, I'm not staying. All I want is that safe deposit key and I'm off again.

Roland You mean it?

Sidney Of course I mean it. I'm very fond of Julia, I wouldn't stand in the way of her new-found happiness.

Roland So you haven't come back to see her?

Sidney No, I'd prefer her to remember me the way I was.

Roland (*cheering up*) Oh then we won't tell her you're alive?

Sidney By far the best.

Roland Oh good.

Sidney Just get the key off her. Where is she?

Roland Oh they're busy for the moment, they're over at the dance organizing things.

Sidney They? Who are they?

Roland Julia and Olivia.

Sidney Olivia? Her mother? *That* Olivia?

Roland Yes that Olivia.

Sidney You mean she's here too?

Roland Yes.

Sidney (*with compassion*) Oh you poor sod. (*He reaches in his pocket*) Have another cigar.

Roland It's a waste of time, she won't let me smoke it, you know what she's like.

Sidney Oh I do. She used to be *my* mother-in-law.

Roland Well if you're alive, she still is.

Sidney And that's another good reason for staying dead.

Roland True. If she knew you were here, she'd be on the phone to the police like a shot.

Sidney Exactly, so let's not waste time. Have you any idea where it is?

Roland I'm trying to think. I wonder if it's in that chest.

They go to the chest of drawers. Sidney kneels down and pulls out the first drawer. He rummages through it, and then pulls out the second drawer. Roland watches as Sidney methodically goes through the odds and ends of buttons, stubs of pencils, etc., contents which accumulate in small drawers

You're very expert, aren't you? Obviously you've had a lot of experience of going through drawers.

Sidney Well of course I have.

Roland What were you. A burglar?

Sidney I was an antique dealer. Hallo, you've got a bit of woodworm here. (*He examines the drawer carefully*)

Roland Oh we haven't, have we?

Sidney Still I don't think it's active. (*He lifts the drawer and sniffs*) No it's been treated. Yes it's been well treated.

Roland Well we've never been cruel to it.

Sidney takes the bottom drawer out completely, lies on the floor and peers into the drawer-space aperture

What are you doing?

Sidney There's a gap at the back, it may have fallen through. (*He feels in the drawer space with his hand*) No, I can't see anything in there. (*He puts the drawer back and is about to get on his feet*)

Olivia enters from the gardens

Olivia Oh Roland, have you ... (*She sees Sidney and stops*)

Sidney lies flat with his face to the floor. He looks like a man about to do press ups

Who's that?

Roland Who's what?

Olivia That man lying on the floor. Who is he?

Roland Oh, you mean this gentleman here. This one.

Olivia Yes that one.

Roland Oh him. He's the woodworm expert.

Olivia But we don't have any woodworm.

Roland Not any more no. But we did have. He's just making sure they've all gone.

Olivia Rubbish, now tell me the truth, who is this man?

Roland Well actually — he came here after the chef's job.

Olivia The chef's job.

Roland Yes.

Olivia (*beckoning Roland to her; sotto voce*) Is he the lunatic who said he was up in a flying saucer?

Roland Yes.

Olivia Then why did you tell me he was a woodworm exterminator?

Roland Because that's what he was — before he became a chef. Now he does a bit of both. Cooks and kills woodworm.

Olivia On a flying saucer?

Roland No no no. He used to work at the Ali Baba Café, cooking and killing woodworm. I met him at the auction sale, and he said he was looking for a job because they'd gone bust and shut down. So I mentioned we might have a vacancy, only of course you would want to interview him. And that's why he phoned earlier.

Olivia Why is he lying on the floor?

Roland I don't know, but he has been out of work — and he may have fainted from hunger.

Olivia Well I think he's drunk.

Roland Oh he can't be, he told me he was a Jehovah's Witness.

Olivia They could tell you anything. The man is a blind drunk and you know it.

Roland All right, perhaps he is.

Olivia Then why couldn't you tell me that in the first place?

Roland Because I thought you might hold me responsible for his condition.

Olivia Were you the one who got him drunk?

Roland Most certainly not. (*Pointing to Sidney*) He was like that when I met him.

Olivia Look at him. Look at the state of him. He must have been drinking since lunch time. (*She bends down to take a closer look at Sidney*)

Roland No, don't get too close, he doesn't like people peering at him when he's passed out. He could turn nasty.

Olivia Well if he's passed out, how can he tell?

Roland He sort of senses it. Like animals do. You know how sleeping dogs growl when you go up to them.

Sidney now gives out a large growl and snarl

I think you've upset him.

Sidney begins to bang the floor with his hands and move his legs jerkily, all the while snarling

Olivia Roland, get him out of here.

Roland Right.

Olivia exits to the garden

Calm down there's a good dog, good boy, down.

Roland crosses to the garden exit to make sure Olivia has gone, then returns to Sidney

It's all right, she's gone.

Sidney rises and brushes himself down

Sidney What a disgusting exhibition of cowardice.

Roland Oh you mustn't blame yourself, Sidney, you couldn't do anything else.

Sidney I'm talking about you.

Roland Me?

Sidney You let that woman walk all over you.

Roland Oh that's charming. I did it for you. I thought you didn't want to be recognized.

Sidney Oh you're right. She'd turn me in to the police as soon as look at me.

Roland Yes, she would.

Sidney So where can I go?

Roland Now where's best — I know, the sauna.

Sidney I don't want a sauna.

Roland No, but you can just sit in there by the plunge pool. It's quite pleasant and I'll go and look for that key.

Vanessa enters from the garden

Vanessa Oh, are you Roland?

Roland Yes.

Vanessa I'm Vanessa Harbinger. Henry's wife.

Roland Oh. How nice to meet you.

Sidney (*resuming his French* accent) So, madame, we meet again. I am Doctor Louis la Roullière.

Vanessa Oh, so you are a doctor.

Sidney brings his heels together, makes a small bow and kisses her hand

Sidney *Enchanté.*

Sidney now gazes into Vanessa's eyes and sets her into a slight flutter

Vanessa I know you speak a little English.

Sidney Oh I do ... *Oui* ... I do speak a little.

Roland Oh of course he do — does. He speaks quite a lot. This lady is the wife — the *femme* ——

Sidney The wife, yes I understand. She is very beautiful. Who is the lucky man who have her?

Roland She is the wife of an old friend of mine, who is very high up in the insurance business. Very high up.

Sidney Oh, the insurance business.

Vanessa My husband is with the Kindly Mutual Insurance Company. You may have heard our slogan "Kindly keep it covered".

Sidney (*after a pause*) Yes, I think I have heard of it.

Roland Oh I'm sure he has.

Vanessa Well, my husband — *mon mari* — he is now the senior claims investigator.

Sidney The claims investigator.
Roland (*slowly and significantly*) Do you understand what she is saying?
Sidney I think I do. Her husband investigates people who have taken money from the insurance company that they are not entitled to have. *N'est ce pas?*
Vanessa Oh bang on. Then he puts them in prison.

Vanessa gives a merry chuckle. Roland and Sidney join in

Sidney Oh very funny — *très amusant.*
Roland Yes, isn't it. Well we mustn't delay the doctor. You mustn't forget your patients, Doctor. *Les* Invalids.
Sidney Ah no. In French *Les Invalides* are not invalids, they are old soldiers.
Vanessa And in England we say old soldiers never die.
Roland Well these will if he doesn't get out there and look at them. Come along, Doctor.

Roland takes Sidney by the arm and they cross to the centre arch

Vanessa *Au revoir,* Doctor.
Sidney *Au revoir, madame.*
Roland I'll be back in a moment.

Roland and Sidney exit UL *to the sauna*

Vanessa looks around. She goes to the spa water dispenser and squirts a little into a paper cup. The tap makes a noise like a ship's siren followed by mild explosions and gurgles, then a tiny squirt of water emerges. Vanessa takes a sip and recoils in disgust

Roland enters from the sauna

Roland Ah, that looks like our sparkling spa water.
Vanessa Yes.
Roland Yes, we recommend you drink two litres of that every day.
Vanessa (*faintly*) Two litres?
Roland Well you can have more if you wish, but that's the minimum.
Vanessa Well I suppose one gets used to it.
Roland Er — no.
Vanessa No?
Roland No, I must be honest. One never actually gets used to it.
Vanessa Why is that?
Roland Well the flavour keeps changing. One day it tastes like burned bicycle tyres, and the next it has a sort of inky taste. You probably remember from school the taste of ink.

Vanessa Oh yes I do.

Roland It's like a lucky dip. In fact last week it tasted like Scotch and soda.

Vanessa Scotch and soda?

Roland Yes, talking of that, where's Henry?

Vanessa Oh he's delayed, he's coming later.

Roland I look forward to seeing him. Keeping well is he?

Vanessa Oh very well, but he keeps putting on weight.

Roland Don't worry we'll soon take that off him.

Vanessa I'm so glad you're friends again.

Roland Well we did have a slight disagreement over — er ...

Vanessa I know, but Henry was never suspicious like some of them were. Oh there were some evil tongues wagging up there at head office.

Roland I can well believe that.

Vanessa One person — I'll name no names — said, "I wouldn't be surprised if her first husband didn't show up one day for his share".

Roland (*alarmed*) Who said that?

Vanessa Never mind who said it. Henry shut them up right away. Do you know what he said?

Roland (*agitated*) What, go on tell me, what?

Vanessa Henry said, "I know Roland Dickerby, and he's not the man to risk fifteen years in prison."

Roland (*cutting in*) Fifteen years? Fifteen *years*?

Vanessa Yes that's what Henry said.

Roland Good God, you don't get fifteen years for doing a thing like that do you?

Vanessa We are talking about criminal conspiracy.

Roland Oh that's if you do it *deliberately*. I mean if it was some sort of plan or scheme to defraud.

Vanessa Well of course, that's what we're talking about.

Roland Well yes, yes of course. I'm glad Henry stuck up for me.

Vanessa He thinks a great deal of you, Roland. He was awfully sorry when you had to resign.

Roland Yes he told me so at the time. When he suggested it.

Vanessa Anyway here you are now, making people fit and well and healthy.

Roland Increasing their lifespan and saving the company a fortune. What time is Henry coming?

Vanessa I said I'd meet him on the half-past ten train.

Roland Oh jolly good, well why don't you pop over to the Midsummer's Dance and join in the festivities.

Vanessa Yes, I may do. On the other hand I may go in the woods and record some bird-song.

Roland Feel free. Go anywhere you wish.

Vanessa I'll see you again later. (*She crosses to the garden exit*)

Julia hurries in from the sauna. She carries a small torch

Hallo.
Julia Hallo.

Vanessa exits to the gardens

Roland, I just went into the sauna to cover up that stuffed camel. There's a man in the plunge pool.
Roland Is there?
Julia Yes?
Roland Did you — er — did you see who he was?
Julia No it's dark in there. I took out the light bulb so Mother wouldn't see the camel. All I had was a torch. Do you think he's fallen in?
Roland Well he may have.
Julia Well who is he?
Roland It's that feller who came after the chef's job. McTavish.
Julia The lunatic on the phone?
Roland Yes.
Julia Well what's he doing in the plunge pool?
Roland Well he asked me if he could freshen up — with a quick dip.
Julia But he's fully dressed, Roland.
Roland Is he? Oh good.
Julia I don't want him here.
Roland No of course not.
Julia Then let's get rid of him.
Roland No. No. I'll do it ...You stay here. I'll go and get rid of him. I'll fire him here and now.
Julia You mean you hired him?
Roland Only for a moment. But don't worry I'll sack him. I'll give him a day's pay in lieu of notice. (*He crosses* UL)

Vanessa enters again from the gardens

Vanessa Me again.
Roland Hallo.
Vanessa You're going to find me an awful nuisance.
Roland Yes — er, no. Not in the least. Do excuse me. This is my wife Julia.
Vanessa Yes we have met.

Roland exits to the sauna

I went to my chalet to get my tape recorder, and the washbasin's leaking.

Julia Oh I am sorry. I thought that was fixed. I'll find you another one. Let's see what we've got left. Not much. Oh here's a nice one, chalet ten. I'll help you move your things.

Vanessa I do hate being a nuisance.

Julia Oh, it's our fault entirely.

Julia takes the key and they exit to the gardens. Roland enters from the sauna and rushes to the office. He enters immediately with an old raincoat which he takes to the sauna

Hooper enters DL and goes to the cupboard. He creeps inside and is slowly closing the door as Roland enters from the sauna. He stops in his tracks when he sees cupboard door moving. He goes over and opens it wide. Hooper immediately steps out again

Roland What are you doing in there?

Hooper No idea.

Roland What do you mean, no idea?

Hooper I'm light-headed from lack of food.

Roland Then go to the treatment room and lie down.

Hooper I just hope I don't collapse on the way. I've been in a daze.

Roland No, you've just been in a cupboard.

Hooper exits DL as Sidney rushes from the sauna clutching the old raincoat around his naked body

Sidney Is this the best you can find me?

Roland For the moment, yes. What the hell did you have to take your clothes off for?

Sidney I was soaked. I dived into the pool to get away from that bloody camel. It tried to bite me.

Roland Don't talk rubbish, it's stuffed.

Sidney Is it? Well someone ought to tell it. I thought it was going to attack me. Now I'm going to get pneumonia.

Roland Just go to chalet ten and have a hot shower. The key's not here. It must be in the door. Just go out the back, turn right, and it's on your left. And whatever you do, don't let anybody see your face.

Roland exits to the office, Sidney exits to the gardens

Hooper enters once again from DL for one last attempt to get at the biscuits. He just opens the cupboard door and there is a loud scream, off

Hooper slams the door shut as Roland comes out of the office carrying a pair of waiter's trousers

Roland Was that you screaming?
Hooper No.
Roland Well who was it?
Hooper No idea. Did you say lie down in the television room?
Roland No, the treatment room.
Hooper The treatment room. Right.

Hooper exits DL

Sidney runs in from the garden. He is out of breath and clutching his raincoat

Sidney Julia was in there.
Roland In where?
Sidney Chalet ten — with that insurance woman.
Roland Did they recognize you?
Sidney No, I don't think so. Where now?
Roland In there, and take these.

Roland hands Sidney the waiter's trousers and bundles him into the cupboard, and shuts the door

Julia enters out of breath

Julia Did he come in here?
Roland Who?
Julia The flasher.
Roland Flasher?

Vanessa runs in from the gardens, also out of breath

Vanessa A wretched man exposed himself to us. He came in the chalet wearing a filthy raincoat.
Julia Then he pulled it up over his head.
Roland Ah. So you didn't see his face?
Vanessa No, that was about all we didn't see.
Roland Could you describe him?
Vanessa I could, but I wouldn't care to.
Julia I was looking the other way. I didn't really see him.
Roland Well it was no big thing.

Vanessa No it wasn't, but I think we should ring the police.
Roland Oh no need for that, good heavens no, I'm sure we can deal with it.
Vanessa Yes, we know who it was.
Roland (*taken aback*) Oh um ah. Do we?
Julia Of course we do, it's that new chef, the one who was in the plunge pool, McTavish.
Roland Ah yes him — yes of course — McTavish.
Vanessa Is that his name? McTavish?
Julia Yes, the man's raving mad. A lunatic.

Olivia enters from the garden

Olivia What's all the commotion about?
Julia Oh, a man exposed himself.

Olivia registers full horror

Roland It's nothing to worry about.
Vanessa Well I think otherwise.
Olivia Now what exactly did he expose?
Roland Good heavens what a question. He showed them his——
Olivia I see, and where was it?
Vanessa Well, where it usually is.
Olivia I mean where did the incident take place.
Julia Chalet ten.
Olivia Then we must find out who it is.
Julia We know who it is: it's the new chef.
Olivia What new chef? Not that woodworm exterminator?
Julia Roland engaged him.
Olivia Oh, I can't believe it.
Julia He's not right in the head.
Olivia You should have thought of that before you married him.
Julia I mean the chef.
Roland All right, so I made a mistake. I'll find him and sack him.
Julia I thought you sacked him.
Roland I did once, yes.
Olivia Well obviously once isn't enough. Find him and sack him again.
Roland I will yes — immediately.
Vanessa I would like to go back to the chalet, if you think that's safe.
Olivia We'll walk back with you. Now where's that walking stick we had? The one with the sharp spike on the end. Is it in the cupboard?
Roland No, not in there no. It's outside in the garden shed.
Olivia Good, we'll pick that up on the way.

Olivia, Julia and Vanessa exit to the garden

Roland walks part of the way with them to make sure they have left, then goes over and opens the cupboard

Sidney is now wearing the waiter's trousers. He holds the carrier bag containing the biscuits

Roland What's that?
Sidney No idea, it was sticking in my back. Where to now?
Roland The office, and put some clothes on.

Roland takes the carrier bag from Sidney who crosses to the office and opens the door

Sidney There's a man in there wearing a red hat and with no trousers.
Roland That's because you're wearing them, it's the dummy.
Sidney Shall I put the rest of his gear on?
Roland Good idea. But don't bother with the hat.

Roland has meanwhile pulled the tin of chocolate wafers from the carrier bag

Sidney What's that?
Roland Mrs Pinkerton's chocolate wafers.
Sidney Well share them out.
Roland Don't be ridiculous. These have been confiscated — and some-
body's opened the tin. (*He takes the lid off the tin and looks at the biscuits*)

Sidney leans over and grabs a biscuit and exits

Put that back. Put that back — at once do you hear me?

Roland tries to open the door, but Sidney holds it from the other side

Open this door — and put that back. You're a thief.

As there is no response from Sidney, Roland gives up. He sighs. He is about to put the lid back on the tin and gazes at the contents. He is obviously tempted. Then he rams the lid back on and takes the tin to reception and puts it on the desk

He walks away, then stops. He succumbs to temptation. He runs back and, taking off the lid of the tin amd starts to cram wafers into his mouth. He moves close to the sofa, still chewing wafers, with his back to the garden

Olivia enters from the gardens, carrying her walking stick

Olivia Roland.

Roland freezes, and blows out a cloud of wafer crumbs. Clutching the biscuit tin he lies on the sofa and rolls over on his stomach with the biscuit tin underneath him

Olivia Roland, what's wrong with you?
Roland Stomach ache.

Olivia comes over and looks at him

Julia comes in from the gardens

Julia What's wrong?
Olivia Roland has stomach ache.
Julia Oh, poor darling.

Julia crosses to the sofa

Is it bad?
Roland Pretty bad. But not too bad. Just leave me alone and I'll be all right.
Olivia He's been in the pub all afternoon, apart from swilling beer heaven knows what trash food he's been eating.
Julia Oh don't nag him, Mother. Not when he's in pain.

Roland gives a deep groan

Olivia I'm sorry, Julia, it's time we had it out. Then he went back in the pub and met that dreadful chef.
Julia I didn't know Roland met him in the pub.
Olivia Where else would he meet him. A sexual pervert. I mean, just imagine him handling the food.
Julia I'd rather not.
Olivia Well one thing has come out of all this. We cannot trust Roland to engage staff.
Roland I don't want to do anything. Just go away and leave me in peace.

Olivia spots a piece of chocolate biscuit on the floor dropped by Roland. She bends down and picks it up

Olivia What's this?

Julia I don't know. What is it?
Olivia It's a chocolate biscuit. Stand up, Roland.
Roland I can't.
Olivia Yes you can.

Olivia stabs Roland on the bottom with the walking stick

Now stand up.

Roland stands up leaving the tin of biscuits on the sofa. Olivia points to the tin with her walking stick

Olivia Mrs Pinkerton's biscuits.
Roland Good heavens, have I been laying on top of that? No wonder I had a stomach ache.

Olivia picks it up, and opens it

Olivia This tin was unopened when I put it in the cupboard, and now it's half empty. You've eaten them.
Roland Me? Why me? It could have been anybody. I mean, the place is full of half starved weirdoes.
Olivia Yes and you're the one who brings them here, and offers them jobs.

There is a loud crash, off, from the office

There's somebody in the office.
Roland *(desperately)* No there isn't. All right I admit everything. I had two chocolate biscuits — I may have had three. You're right, Olivia, I'm a chocoholic.

Olivia and Julia ignore him. Their attention is focused on the office door. There is another crash, off

Julia What's going on in there?
Roland Nothing.

Roland snatches the tin of biscuits and, tearing it open, begins cramming them into his mouth

Look at me. Look at me. I'm a chocoholic. I need help.
Olivia *(ignoring him)* It's probably that wretch who exposed himself. *(She raises her walking stick and bangs on the door with it)* Come out of there,

come out. Do you hear me? *(She bangs on the door again)* And if you do it again, I shall skewer you.

Pause

Finally, the door opens and Sidney enters. He is wearing the rest of the waiter's suit taken from the dummy. He wears old scruffy carpet slippers. He has sunglasses on and a handkerchief held over his mouth. To explain this, he comes forward half doubled up in a series of racking coughs. When not coughing, he groans and gasps for breath

Julia Is that McTavish?
Roland *(cutting in)* No of course it isn't. That was the chef.
Olivia Is that the wretch who exposes himself?
Roland Well he hasn't so far.
Julia Then who is he?

Olivia prods Sidney in the back with her stick

Olivia Who are you?
Roland Don't poke him like that, you could do him an injury.
Olivia I merely asked him who he was.
Roland He doesn't speak English.
Olivia Then you know him?
Roland Of course I know him — he's our head waiter.
Julia Our *what*?
Roland The new head waiter. He used to be head waiter at the Ali Baba Café.
Olivia Oh I don't believe it. Do you mean to say you've engaged *him* as well?
Roland Yes.
Olivia But why?
Roland I thought he'd give the place a touch of class.

Sidney goes into another paroxysm of coughing. Then he takes off his slipper and scratches his foot. His sock has a large hole in it. He replaces the carpet slipper and starts to cough again

Olivia Have you looked at him? Look at those carpet slippers.
Roland Well I mean, he's off duty. He's been on his feet all day. I told him he could have the evening off and now all you do is insult him and poke him with your walking stick.
Olivia A moment ago you said he didn't speak English.
Roland No. But he understands it.
Olivia Then tell him to clear off.

Roland (*in horror*) Do what?

Olivia Get rid of him, Roland, and while you're at it, any other riff raff you've hired from the Ali Baba Café.

Roland There was only him and the chef. He'll be very upset, he had his heart set on working here.

Olivia Then we'll leave you to break the news to him — and in the future do not hire staff without seeing me. Is that clear?

Roland Perfectly. It means you have reduced my role in this establishment to that of a meaningless cypher: without authority, dignity — or purpose.

Olivia Precisely.

Olivia pushes Sidney out of her way with her walking stick and, together with Julia, exits to the gardens

Sidney waits for a moment before straightening up

Roland Oh God, that was a narrow squeak.

Sidney It's been one narrow squeak after another. Have you found that key yet?

Roland Key? What key?

Sidney The key to the safe deposit you great half-witted idiot. The reason I came here.

Roland Look, why don't you just go away for a while, and we'll forward the key on to you. After we give the money back.

Sidney (*horrified*) Give the money back?

Roland That money is being returned to its rightful owners. The Kindly Mutual Insurance Company.

Sidney You're not going mad, are you?

Roland No, and I'm not going to prison either.

Sidney How are you going to give the money back without telling them I'm alive?

Roland Well, I'll just say we don't want it any more.

Sidney They're not idiots. They'll smell a rat. They'll guess I'm alive and if I'm alive do you know what that means?

Roland Yes, you won't be dead.

Sidney And Julia won't be married to you. She will be married to me.

Roland She can divorce you.

Sidney And supposing she doesn't want to? Supposing she wants to come back to me.

Roland Oh of course she won't ... (*He is suddenly struck by doubts*) I mean she doesn't — she wouldn't. Oh, of course she wouldn't. I know she wouldn't — oh, of course she wouldn't.

Sidney Well, let's just tell her I'm alive and see.

Roland (*shouting*) No. I er — know she won't. I mean she doesn't even like
  you.
Sidney How do you know?
Roland Because she's told me so, lots of times.
Sidney You mustn't believe everything that a woman tells you.
Roland Julia and I love each other.
Sidney Of course you do — and I don't want to take her away from you.
  Unless you force me. Do you follow me?
Roland Yes.
Sidney Good. Now keep your big mouth shut, and find me the key.

Sidney exits to the office and shuts the door

Roland gives a deep sigh and exits DL *as Vanessa enters from the gardens.
She carries a small tape recorder*

Vanessa Oh Mr Dickerby. Is anybody about?

*Vanessa goes to the office and taps on the door. Then she opens it and peers
in. She gives a scream and staggers back. Then grabs the door handle and
pulls it shut. She holds on to the handle for dear life*

  Help, somebody help me — help.

Roland runs in from DL

  That monster McTavish is back, he's in there stark naked. Only now he's
  wearing a red hat.
Roland Was he wearing it on his head?
Vanessa Yes. Where else would he wear it? He was standing with his back
  to me.
Roland Well don't worry, I shan't permit him to harm you.

Vanessa lets go of the door handle and backs away

Vanessa Wretched man. I can't think what possesses them.
Roland Perhaps they get frustrated.
Vanessa Frustrated? They ought to be — incarcerated.
Roland (*sadly*) Yes, once I thought as you do. Until I got to know McTavish.
  Now I have nothing but sympathy.
Vanessa Sympathy?
Roland Apart from that minor aberration, McTavish is one of the finest
  human beings I have ever known.

Vanessa (*impressed*) Really? In what way?

Roland That man — that man in there, with the red hat on. Has just spent five years in Madagascar.

Vanessa What doing?

Roland He ran some sort of clinic — an animal clinic.

Vanessa For sick animals?

Roland And birds, especially birds.

Vanessa Oh, did he really? I'm recording bird-song you know. I'm awfully fond of birds.

Roland And so is McTavish. He was once known as the birdman of Madagascar.

Vanessa Is he a practising ornithologist?

Roland Not any more no. Not since he had the accident.

Vanessa Accident?

Roland The one which left him, as you see him today, a pathetic wreck of his former self.

Vanessa But what happened to him?

Roland Well, it would seem he was trying to rescue an injured pigeon.

Vanessa Where from?

Roland From the top of an enormous coconut tree — a gigantic coconut tree, eighty feet high.

Vanessa Eighty feet high?

Roland Yes. He got on the top, rescued the pigeon and was on the way down when it happened.

Vanessa What did?

Roland He was struck on the head by a falling coconut.

Vanessa How dreadful. Was he wearing his hat?

Roland No. It fell off and so did he. He crashed to the ground unconscious.

Vanessa And what happened to the pigeon?

Roland Oh the pigeon.

Vanessa The injured pigeon, what happened to it?

Roland Ah this is the point. McTavish tucked the pigeon under his raincoat, that same raincoat you saw him wear earlier. He carried it under his raincoat, until it recovered.

Vanessa How extraordinary.

Roland Yes, he made a sort of sling for it, which hung around his neck, and as it grew stronger and learned to fly again, he would open his raincoat and off it would go — soaring and circling among the clouds into the great blue sky.

Vanessa Oh how lovely.

Roland Until one day — one day, sadly, it never came back.

Vanessa But why does he expose himself?

Roland I'm coming to that, you see the blow on his head from the coconut made him absent-minded. He forgets all manner of things. Sometimes he forgets to put his trousers on — and then he is walking along absent mindedly, and suddenly — he remembers the pigeon he once had. He throws open his raincoat. To the world he is exposing himself, but in McTavish's poor clouded brain, he is letting his pigeon out.

Vanessa What an extraordinary story.

Roland Yes, isn't it.

Vanessa Can you vouch for its authenticity?

Roland Well, I had it from the doctor who treats McTavish.

Vanessa Then he is under medical supervision?

Roland Oh indeed he is, yes a specialist. A French doctor. I wonder you didn't see him in there with McTavish.

Vanessa Oh dear, I didn't stop to look, there may have been somebody in there with him.

Roland I'm sure there was. We try now never to leave McTavish alone. I'll check. (*He taps on the office door*) Oh, Doctor. Doctor Louis.

Sidney opens door cautiously. He is wearing a white coat

Sidney I have found one of your white coats. You don't mind.

Roland No, Doctor. (*Going to introduce Vanessa*) This is ... Oh, of course you've already met.

Vanessa We have.

Sidney *Oui.*

Roland This is McTavish's doctor. You can go back now. We were just checking.

Vanessa No wait. He won't do it again will he?

Sidney points to Roland

Sidney Why, what have you done?

Vanessa No, not Roland. McTavish.

Sidney Ah McTavish.

Vanessa They obviously didn't tell you, but he walked into our chalet and threw open his raincoat and — oh dear, it was horrible. The most revolting thing I have ever seen.

Roland Was it?

Vanessa Oh, it was.

Sidney (*coldly*) Well of course, that is just your opinion.

Vanessa Ugly beyond belief.

Sidney Quiet, madame, please. He may be listening. Do you want to give him an inferiority complex?

Vanessa I'm sorry, I was carried away, I know he can't help it. I know he is letting his pigeon out.
Sidney His what?
Vanessa His pigeon. But it was revolting.
Sidney That's enough, madame.
Roland (*looking around nervously*) Yes, I think you should go in now. He may break loose.
Sidney Stand back, madame, in case he fly at you.
Vanessa You think he might?
Sidney If he hear what you say about his — his pigeon I would not be surprised.

Vanessa moves nervously away from the door. Sidney opens it a fraction and shouts inside

Stand back, McTavish. Stand back, I say.

Sidney opens the door and runs inside, then slams it

Roland There you are. The doctor has him under control.
Vanessa I do hope so. Tell me, have you ever thought about getting him another pigeon.
Roland Another pigeon?
Vanessa It may help — especially if he carried it outside his raincoat.
Roland Oh. On his shoulder?
Vanessa Possibly.
Roland I will certainly give it a great deal of thought.

Roland and Vanessa exit DL, *as Hooper enters from the gardens*

Hooper creeps to the cupboard and opens the door and searches for the shopping bag. He grows more frantic. He pulls odds and ends out of the cupboard, including a beekeeper's helmet

Julia enters from the gardens

Julia Mr Hooper, what *are* you doing here?
Hooper Nothing. I er — happened to be passing the cupboard when the door fell open, and all this stuff fell out. I'm trying to put it back.
Julia Oh dear, I am sorry. I'll help you. (*She starts to put stuff back*)
Hooper Isn't that a beekeeper's helmet?
Julia Yes.
Hooper I didn't know you kept bees?

Julia Yes, we've got six hives behind the shrubbery. We produce all our own honey.

Hooper How nice, and who eats that?

Julia Well, it wouldn't be on your slimming diet ...

Hooper No of course it wouldn't. It's the other lot, isn't it?

Julia Perhaps when you've lost some more weight.

Hooper Yes.

Julia stows the last half of the stuff in the cupboard and shuts the door

I'll be off then.

Julia starts to exit DL *and Hooper starts to exit to the gardens*

Julia goes

Hooper runs back and opens the cupboard and starts rummaging again

They've gone, somebody had them — somebody's had those biscuits.

Hooper finds the beekeeper's helmet again. He takes it out, puts it on, and exits to the gardens, as Roland enters DL

Roland sees the cupboard door left open. He goes over and shuts it and the spa water makes a noise like an intermittent ship siren. He fiddles with the tap

Sidney opens the office door and peers out

Sidney What's making all the noise? It's not you, is it?

Roland It's the spa water.

Sidney Well if I were you, I wouldn't drink it.

Sidney goes back into the office as Olivia hurries in from the sauna

Olivia Roland, quickly, I need your help.

Roland Why, what's wrong?

Olivia I went into the sauna with a torch. There was a camel in there.

Roland A camel? Oh, a camel.

Olivia I thought it was going to bite me, so I pushed it into that plunge pool. I think it's drowning.

Roland No, it's swimming. Camels can swim.

Olivia Roland, that camel is drowning. It sank like a stone.

Roland No, camels like swimming underwater. Just leave it.
Olivia Roland, will you please come and help me pull it out?
Roland No, Olivia.
Olivia Why not?
Roland Have you ever tried to lift a camel?
Olivia No.
Roland The average camel weighs half a ton — give or take a hundred weight — and that's a *dry* camel. Have you ever thought what a wet camel weighs?
Olivia No, and I don't care. But I can't watch a poor creature drown.
Roland Then don't look at it.
Olivia My God, but you're callous.

Olivia exits hurriedly to the sauna

Roland goes to the office and knocks on the door

Roland It's me.

Sidney opens the door and peers out

Sidney Found that key yet?
Roland No. But I've been thinking. If I am to help you, Sidney, if I am to keep you out of prison — it's on one condition.
Sidney What's that?
Roland That Julia never ever finds out you're alive.
Sidney That's all right, and what about the insurance money?
Roland We'll wait until you've gone back to Madagascar and then I'll find some way of returning it. I don't know how yet. Now go back in the office.

They have moved a distance from the office. Sidney turns to go back in again

Julia runs in from the sauna

Julia Quickly, it's Mother.

Sidney freezes, his back to Julia

Roland Why, what's happened?
Julia She's slipped into the plunge pool.
Roland Well don't panic, Julia, we'll haul her out.
Julia But she's trapped under that camel — caught up in the harness. We'll need help.

Sidney dives into the office and shuts the door

Who's that man?
Roland Nobody. Ignore him.
Julia But we need him, Roland, we need help.

She tries to go into the office, but Roland holds her back

Hooper runs in from the gardens wearing the beekeeper's helmet

Hooper All your bees are loose. There's bees everywhere. Bees bees bees.
Roland Oh bugger the bees.

Vanessa runs in from the sauna

Vanessa Your mother-in-law is being drowned by a camel.
Roland Yes I know, we're coming. Come on, Hooper.

Led by Vanessa, Roland and Hooper exit to the sauna, leaving Julia to follow them. But instead she runs into the office

After a second she screams, off, staggers out of the office and collapses

CURTAIN

ACT II

The same. Ten minutes later

When the Curtain *rises, Julia and Roland are sitting on the sofa. They are both somewhat subdued. There is a pause*

Julia I'd like to see him, Roland.

Roland But you *have* seen him.

Julia I mean properly.

Roland Why? What's the point?

Julia I don't know. I just want to *see* him.

Roland Julia, you saw him — and then you fainted.

Julia Well so would anybody. I just want to ask him what happened.

Roland He's a bad lot, Julia.

Julia I know he is. But I was married to him for three years. I can't just let him come back — and disappear without even speaking to him.

Roland I don't see why. Anyway, he doesn't want to see you.

Julia How do you know?

Roland He told me.

Julia I've only your word for that.

Roland Well, isn't that enough for you? The word of your lawfully wedded husband.

Julia But you're not now are you. Sidney is.

Roland (*after a pause*) Only if you know he's alive.

Julia But I *do* know he's alive.

Roland Yes, but nobody knows you know he's alive — and so long as nobody knows you know he's alive, nobody knows that you know you're not married to me.

Julia Can you say that again?

Roland No.

Julia Does Mother know he's alive? ·

Roland No. Not yet.

Julia Shall we tell her?

Roland Not until we have to.

Julia When will that be?

Roland I suppose when we give the insurance money back.

Julia Give it back? What do you mean? (*Horror*) *Give it back?*

Roland Just give it back.

Julia But how can we give it back? We've spent it.

Roland Well, it won't be easy.

Julia But why do we have to give it back?

Roland Because if we keep it and they find out Sidney is alive, we can go to prison for fifteen years.

Julia But that's only if they can *prove* we know he's alive.

Roland Right, and at the moment they can't *prove* you know he's alive. You just caught a brief glimpse of somebody that looked like him — and then you fainted.

Julia Yes, that's true. You're right, maybe it's best if I don't see him.

Roland Of course it is. Now give me a kiss and run off and find that key.

Julia kisses him and exits DL

Roland goes towards the office

Sidney opens the door and comes out

Roland She doesn't want to see you.

Sidney Well no. Not now you've talked her out of it.

Roland Oh, you were listening.

Sidney Well of course I was listening — and she wanted to see me desperately.

Roland You couldn't have been listening very hard if you think that. Anyway, I thought you didn't want to see *her*.

Sidney At one point, yes — but that was before she fainted and I gave her the kiss of life.

Roland When?

Sidney While you were fishing Olivia out of the pool. I did it to bring her round. But suddenly it all came back to me. Those happy days when we were first married. The feel of her ——

Roland (*cutting in*) Stop it. How dare you.

Sidney How dare I what?

Roland How dare you feel my wife's ... whatever it was you felt.

Sidney I was about to say her proximity.

Roland Oh, were you? Well just remember, she is my wife, and you took advantage of her while she was unconscious.

Sidney She's not your wife, she's mine, and furthermore what makes you think she was unconscious?

Roland You foul-mouthed filthy swine, Sidney. You are rotten through and through. You are unspeakably yuk. That's what you are. Yuk.

Sidney Now watch it, Roland. I'm not trying to take her away from you. I'm just worried that Julia may want to come back to me.

Roland She wouldn't come back to you if you were the last man on earth.

Sidney That's what she says, but how will she act? You never know with women. I think she's at the crossroads. Who shall it be? You or me? You see, Roland, when I held her in my arms, I was the one who had to break free. She clung to me.

Roland She was unconscious.

Sidney All right, but remember this. If you tell that insurance company I'm alive before I get away from here, I shall no longer restrain her affection for me — and you will have lost her forever. Now go and find me that key.

Roland And you stay away from Julia's proximity.

Roland exits DL

Sidney spots a biscuit on the floor. He picks it up and looks at it and blows fluff off it

Vanessa enters from the garden, carrying her tape recorder

Vanessa Ah, Doctor, you'll be glad to know Olivia has recovered. She is upstairs drying her hair.

Sidney Ah good.

Vanessa But the camel, poor creature, is no more. It lies at the bottom of the plunge pool.

Sidney How ironic, madame. For a camel to end this way, when they go so long without water.

Vanessa Tragic. I wonder, could I see McTavish?

Sidney (*horrified*) See him?

Vanessa I mean if he's fully dressed.

Sidney No, madame, that is impossible.

Roland enters DL

Roland Now then, Doctor, nothing is impossible.

Sidney She wants to see McTavish.

Roland Ah now that *is* impossible. Why do you want to see him?

Vanessa I feel I may be able to help him.

Roland But he's a sex maniac — how could you help him?

Sidney coughs and whistles

Vanessa Well, we have a common interest in ornithology.

Sidney Oh. The ornithology.

Vanessa And I thought that perhaps if I were to play him some bird-song——

Roland Bird-song?

Vanessa Oh yes. There's all sorts here. (*She taps her tape recorder*) I have a lark mating.

Roland Oh I'm sure you do. But not with him you wouldn't.

Sidney I must go and attend him. *Excusez-moi.*

Sidney goes into the office and closes the door. There is a sound of crashing, and Sidney pokes his head out

Vanessa is trying to peer into the office

Stand back, madame, stand clear.

Vanessa (*standing back*) Oh dear, is he really that violent?

Sidney I have never known him like this before. He is like a raging tiger.

Sidney goes into the office as Olivia enters DL

Olivia Oh, Roland.

Roland Yes, Olivia. How are you feeling?

Olivia Oh I expect I shall be all right. I'll just sit down for a moment. (*She sits on the sofa*) Could you just go over to the dance and see what's happening? It should be the interval shortly, and I don't feel quite up to it.

Roland Yes, of course.

Roland exits to the gardens

Vanessa You've had a dreadful shock.

Olivia I know, I just cannot imagine what that camel was doing in the sauna.

Vanessa I suppose it must have escaped from somewhere.

Olivia Yes. I do wish people would look after their animals. Stray cats are bad enough, but camels.

Vanessa You look quite pale, perhaps Doctor Louis should see you.

Olivia Doctor Louis? Who is Doctor Louis?

Vanessa A specialist in nervous disorders. He's in there examining McTavish.

Olivia Where did he come from?

Vanessa Roland got him. He's from Madagascar.

Olivia Madagascar? Couldn't he find one closer?

Vanessa Apparently he's been treating McTavish for years.

Olivia And who's paying the bill?

Vanessa I've no idea.

Vanessa exits DL *as Woman Police Sergeant Campbell enters from the gardens. Sergeant Campbell is a smart attractive young woman with a slight Scots' accent. She has a businesslike but somewhat deadpan approach. She is dressed in police uniform*

Olivia recognizes her and rises

Sgt Campbell Oh, Mrs de Vere, I've been looking for you everywhere.

Olivia Oh it's Sergeant Campbell, isn't it? You're in charge of the band.

Sgt Campbell I'm the road manager.

Olivia Oh well, whatever you call it. Is it the interval?

Sgt Campbell Yes, and I'm afraid we have some trouble.

Olivia Not — hooliganism?

Sgt Campbell Oh no, nothing like that. They're all very well behaved.

Olivia Yes, we don't give them any meat. It keeps down the animal passions. So what happened?

Sgt Campbell Somebody has opened the back of our minibus and taken a wicker hamper.

Olivia A wicker hamper?

Sgt Campbell Containing (*she pulls out her notebook*) the band's refreshments. Namely twelve beef sandwiches, twenty-four ham sandwiches, four chicken legs, a dozen doughnuts and twelve cans of beer.

Olivia Oh that's outrageous.

Sgt Campbell It's not what we expect when we perform to an audience of vegetarians.

Olivia Have you any idea who took it?

Sgt Campbell Police Constable Hobson, who plays on clarinet and doubles on banjo, thought he saw a beekeeper loitering.

Olivia But we haven't got a beekeeper.

Sgt Campbell Well, he was wearing a beekeeper's helmet and hovering near the minibus.

Olivia Possibly he put that on so he wouldn't be recognized.

Sgt Campbell More than likely. But who is it?

Olivia Well, we've had a very motley crew here looking for work. They came from the Ali Baba Café.

Sgt Campbell (*meaningfully*) Oh, the Ali Baba Café.

Olivia Do you know it?

Sgt Campbell Oh I do, a hotbed of thieves.

Olivia Was it? Well, it must be one of those. It could have been the head waiter, or the chef — yes *that's* who it was. The chef McTavish.

Sgt Campbell Is he still about?

Olivia I'm told he's in the office being examined by his doctor. What's the legal position on medical fees in Madagascar?

Sgt Campbell I've no idea.

Olivia I'd better go over to the dance and see what's happening.

Sgt Campbell Yes, fine. Oh, by the way, the band want to know, who is giving out the fancy-dress prizes.
Olivia I am. Dressed as Titania.
Sgt Campbell Titania?
Olivia Yes, Titania, the Fairy Queen. It's midsummer's night.
Sgt Campbell Oh, of course, yes — and whose idea was that?
Olivia Mine. But I don't really feel up to it. I suppose you wouldn't like to dress up and do it for me?
Sgt Campbell No, I think I'll wait around and speak to McTavish.

Olivia exits to the gardens

Sergeant Campbell goes over to look at the water dispenser and helps herself to a drink. The water fountain makes a subdued noise

Hooper, wearing the beekeeper's helmet and carrying the hamper, runs in from DL

Sergeant Campbell doesn't notice

Hooper very slowly tiptoes backwards out again

(*After sipping the water*) Oh quite refreshing.

Vanessa enters from the gardens

Vanessa Oh hallo.
Sgt Campbell Hallo.
Vanessa Have you come about McTavish?
Sgt Campbell Yes, I'm waiting here to have a word with him.
Vanessa He's in there being examined.
Sgt Campbell So I am told.
Vanessa He's your man of course. I saw him do it.
Sgt Campbell Did you? What exactly was it you saw?
Vanessa Well, what can I say? He lifted up his raincoat, and there it was.
Sgt Campbell The wicker hamper.
Vanessa The what?
Sgt Campbell The wicker hamper. You saw the wicker hamper.
Vanessa Is that some kind of dialect term for it?
Sgt Campbell I wouldn't have thought so. Wouldn't you call it a wicker hamper where you come from?
Vanessa No, I would not.
Sgt Campbell Well, what would you call it?

Vanessa Does it really matter?

Sgt Campbell No, not really. I'm just being curious. I suppose there couldn't
be two of them could there?

Vanessa Two of them?

Sgt Campbell The one you saw, did it look rather frayed around the edges
— as if it had been knocked about?

Vanessa I didn't examine it all that closely.

Sgt Campbell Well, did you notice it had a piece of old rope around it, sort
of holding it together?

Vanessa No, I did not.

Sgt Campbell And is that all you can tell me?

Vanessa All I can tell you is, he exposed himself.

Sgt Campbell Oh, he did that as well?

Vanessa As well as what?

Sgt Campbell As well as stealing our wicker hamper.

Vanessa I think we must be at cross purposes.

Sgt Campbell I think we must be.

Vanessa What did you want him for?

Sgt Campbell Somebody stole a wicker hamper full of food.

Vanessa You know, it doesn't sound like McTavish.

Sgt Campbell Then perhaps we're on the wrong track.

They cross towards the gardens exit

Vanessa Yes, perhaps we are.

Sgt Campbell He was wearing a beekeeper's helmet.

Vanessa Ah now that's a clue, let's see what we can find. I rather fancy
myself as Miss Marple.

Vanessa and the Sergeant exit to the gardens

Hooper enters DL. *He is still wearing the beekeeper's helmet, and is now
slightly drunk. Briefly lifting his helmet, he looks around the lounge and
then goes back out again. He returns immediately without the helmet, but
carrying the wicker hamper*

*He looks around again and puts the hamper on the reception desk. He
removes two cans of beer, and stows them in his tracksuit. He takes a plastic
wrapped pack of sandwiches and a bag of doughnuts. He stands for a while
taking a bite out of a sandwich and a bite out of a doughnut, alternately. He
stows the remains of the snack in his tracksuit and hides the hamper in the
cupboard. Feeling more secure now, he takes a paper cup from the dispenser,
pours beer into it, and starts drinking the beer*

Julia enters DL

Julia Oh, you seem to be enjoying it.
Hooper I am. It's lovely.
Julia Oh good. Try and drink at least two litres.
Hooper Oh I'm working on it. Cheers.

Hooper exits to the gardens

Julia goes to the reception desk, still looking for the key

Sidney comes out of the office and notices her

Sidney Julia.
Julia Oh, Sidney.
Sidney Let me look at you.
Julia It's better I don't see you. (*She turns her back to him*)
Sidney Why?
Julia Because it is. That's why.
Sidney Oh come on, Julia ——
Julia No, go away.

Sidney comes up behind her and puts his arms around her waist

Hooper enters from the gardens

They don't see him

Sidney Oh come on, darling, how about a kiss for old time's sake?

They both turn and see Hooper

Hooper Oh sorry, don't mind me.

Hooper turns and goes back to the gardens

Julia, breaking free, turns to face Sidney

Julia Why Sidney, why? Why didn't you write and let me know that you
were alive?
Sidney I'm sorry, I know it was a shock. I know you must have been
heartbroken.
Julia Heartbroken?

Sidney Well, weren't you?

Julia Do you know what Mother said when we buried you?

Sidney What?

Julia She said that'll be the first night in three years we know where he is.

Sidney Well that was your mother. What about you?

Julia I agreed with her.

Sidney You've grown hard, Julia. Hard and callous. Whatever happened to that sweet loving girl I used to know?

Julia If you mean Sharon what'sername, she married a greengrocer.

Sidney How did you find out about her?

Julia She turned up at the funeral. Along with the barmaid from the *Rose and Crown* and two other girls I'd never even seen.

Sidney Well, it's been nice seeing you again. I shall always treasure those three happy years we spent together.

Julia At least three weeks of which you spent at home.

Sidney I know now how you really feel about me, Julia, and I admire the way you keep it hidden.

Julia Sidney, I just realized how much I dislike you. Now get away from me.

Sidney Just one farewell kiss.

Sidney takes her hand and pulls her to him

Julia brings her knee up into his groin. He releases her and gives a deep groan before doubling up

He staggers off to the gardens and exits

Olivia enters from DL, *carrying a plastic bag*

Julia Oh Mother, you know those things we found in Sidney's safe deposit?

Olivia Yes, dear.

Julia Do you know what happened to them?

Olivia They were in a cardboard box somewhere. Why do you ask?

Julia Oh nothing. It's just that Roland met a locksmith who said he might know where the safe deposit key belonged.

Olivia Well never mind now, dear, I was wondering if you'd be a fairy queen and give away the prizes. I don't feel up to it.

Julia I'd like to find that key.

Olivia Well you do the fairy queen and I'll go and look for the key. There's the costume.

Olivia hands Julia the plastic bag

Julia Will it fit me?
Olivia Well if it doesn't, we'll pin it up.

*Julia goes into the office with the plastic bag. Olivia exits DL, as Hooper
comes in from the gardens. He looks around and makes for the cupboard.
He opens it and goes inside it, as Roland enters from the gardens, and sees
the door closing. Roland goes across and opens the cupboard door.
Hooper steps out*

Roland You're in there again.
Hooper So what? Look, Dickerby, why do you keep following me around,
harassing me?
Roland Because I want to know what you're up to.
Hooper Well I wouldn't worry what *I'm* up to. I'd worry what your wife is
up to.
Roland What? What do you mean?
Hooper Your wife and that French doctor. I walked in and caught them at
it.

Hooper now makes his way to the gardens. Roland follows him

Roland What do you mean "at it"?
Hooper I've said enough.
Roland No you haven't. Come back here, Mr Hooper. Come back.

*Hooper exits to the gardens and Roland hurries after him. Sidney enters,
still limping, from DL*

He goes across and enters the office, shutting the door

*Roland runs back from the gardens. He looks around and hurries to the
office. He opens the door, and goes in. There is a pause, and then he comes
out again. He looks completely shattered. He staggers away from the door,
a broken man*

*Sidney comes out of the office, followed by Julia in her underwear and
holding the fairy queen dress which she was about to put on*

Roland Oh, Julia. Julia, how could you?
Julia I was changing, Roland.
Roland Yes, changing me for him.
Sidney Now listen to me, Roland.
Roland I don't need to listen. I've seen and heard enough. Don't worry, Julia,
I shan't stand in your way.

Julia Roland, don't be stupid.
Roland Stupid I may be, but not blind. All right, Sidney, you've won, she's all yours.

Roland hurries to the gardens and exits

Julia (*shouting after him*) Roland, come back here. Roland ... Sidney, go after him.
Sidney If you want him *you* go after him.

Julia starts to put on the fairy queen dress

Julia I can't go after him half-dressed. Go after him.
Sidney I don't know why you want him back, he's an idiot.
Julia (*struggling to put on the dress*) He may be an idiot, but he's worth ten of you. Now go after him.
Sidney All right, all right, I'm going.

Sidney takes his time, but ambles off after Roland

Julia manages to get her dress on, and is about to follow

Olivia enters DL

Olivia Oh you've got into it.
Julia Yes, and I'm coming out of it.

Julia tries to go after Roland but Olivia holds her back by her wings

Olivia Never mind, the band's waiting.
Julia Let go, Mother, I've got to see Roland.
Olivia You can see him later, now come on.

Olivia drags Julia out, and they exit to the gardens, as Sidney and Roland enter DL

Sidney I was pulling your leg, Roland, she doesn't want to come back to me. You're the one she wants.
Roland So you say, but I don't trust you. I wouldn't trust you as far as I could throw you.
Sidney Then ask her yourself — ask Julia.

They go to the office, and look inside

Roland She's not in there.

Sidney Well she's gone looking for you. She wants to explain what happened.

Roland What was she doing in that office with you, in her underwear?

Sidney Changing her dress.

Roland I don't believe you.

Sidney All right, don't believe me. Ask her.

Roland It's not just that, Hooper said he saw you kissing her.

Sidney Well Hooper's a liar. Who are you going to believe, Hooper or me?

Roland Oh God, what a choice. Oooh. *(He is suddenly hit by a pain in the back of the neck. He clasps it)*

Sidney What's up now.

Roland It's my neck, and all down my shoulder. *(He sits in the Windsor chair)* I haven't had a moment's peace since you turned up, and now I've pulled a muscle or something.

Sidney That's tension.

Roland And can you wonder at it? It's caused by guilt — that's what that is. Guilt.

Sidney Why, what have you done?

Roland I haven't done anything. I have never done anything wrong in my life. And now I'm being drawn by you into a life of crime.

Sidney Oh you'll get used to it. Just relax.

Roland I don't want to get used to it. Oooh, my neck.

Sidney Perhaps I can massage it for you.

Sidney stands behind Roland and starts to gently massage and pummel his shoulder

Roland I don't care what you say, we have to give that money back.

Sidney Then you'll lose Julia.

Roland *(tragically)* I've already lost her.

Sidney *(brightly)* No you haven't.

Roland Oh yes I have. You double-crossed me, Sidney. You promised you would keep away from her.

Sidney All I did was ——

Roland I don't want to hear what you did. You have obviously resumed your conjugal rights, and that's enough for me.

Sidney Oh don't be an idiot.

Roland As soon as Henry Harbinger gets here, I'm going to tell him the truth.

Sidney And what about me?

Roland I'm not worried about you.

Sidney *(annoyed)* So you don't care if I go to prison?

Roland No, I don't — as long as I don't go.

Sidney My God you're selfish.
Roland Selfish?
Sidney (*angrily*) Yes, you're a selfish pig that's what you are — and I could throttle you.

Sidney takes his hands away from Roland's shoulders and holds them in a pre-throttling position

Vanessa enters from the gardens

Roland Just be careful.
Vanessa Anything wrong?
Roland Yes, Vanessa, I want to tell you the truth.

He is unable to continue as at this point Sidney grabs his head with both hands and gives it a sharp jerk and twist. Roland gives out a cry of pain

Vanessa The truth?
Sidney (*in French accent*) Yes he wants to tell you he is in a great deal of pain.

Sidney has Roland's head in a vice-like grip and is twisting it about

  Isn't that the truth?
Roland (*screaming*) Yes.
Vanessa What's wrong with him, Doctor?
Roland (*screaming*) Doctor, my foot.
Sidney Oh you have hurt your foot as well?
Vanessa Oh dear, he does seem in a bad way.
Sidney I'm afraid he is, madame.

Sidney has Roland's head still in a vice-like grip and twisted to one side. He gives a sudden jerk. Roland yells again

  Was that painful?
Roland Yes. What are you doing?
Sidney I'm checking your vocal reflexes.
Vanessa Why is that?

Sidney now lets go of Roland's head and grabs him around the throat with both hands. Roland gives out a gurgling and choking sounds as he struggles to free Sidney's grip around his throat

Sidney Can you hear that noise he is making?

Vanessa Yes.
Sidney It's a spasm of the lower larynx.
Vanessa Oh. It's a spasm of the lower larynx.
Sidney Yes. I am trying to massage it free.

There is a pause. Vanessa watches for a while with interest

Vanessa It looks as if you're strangling him.
Sidney Yes, to the untrained eye — it would.
Vanessa Yes.
Sidney But it's larynxial massage.
Vanessa Is there any way I can help?
Sidney Yes. Find me some rope.
Vanessa Rope?
Sidney Cord or straps, anything that we have to tie him to the chair.
Vanessa Why?
Sidney Because he may have convulsions. You see how he struggles for breath. Look out the back door. There may be a clothes line hanging. But hurry, madame, we have not much time.

Vanessa runs and exits DL

Sidney relaxes his grip on Roland's throat

Roland You've choked me.
Sidney It's your own stupid fault.

Roland goes to stand up and Sidney puts a hand on either shoulder and pushes him down

Roland You won't stop me talking.
Sidney Now listen. All I want is that key and a chance to get away from here. Is that unreasonable?
Roland Yes.

Vanessa runs in with what looks like an armful of washing

Vanessa I've got it.

Roland tries to stand up. Sidney forces him back into the chair and puts hands round his throat again

Sidney You have bring in the washing?

Vanessa No, it's the clothes line. We can use these.

Vanessa pulls a pair of ladies tights off the clothes line and proceeds to tie Roland up

Sidney Feet first.

Vanessa kneels and ties Roland's feet to the chair

Yes. *Oui*. Very good. I think with luck we may be able to pull him round.
Vanessa Oh I'm so glad. What's wrong with him exactly?
Sidney It is a form of deadly tropical fever.
Vanessa But he couldn't have caught it here could he? I mean it's a health farm.
Sidney Now. I am going to stop the massage and see what happen: don't speak for a moment — and don't worry, if anything goes wrong, I can always start it again.
Vanessa Yes.

Sidney releases his grip. Roland gasps for air, and gives a few deep groans

Roland All right. What do you want me to do?
Sidney Do you feel your vocal chords are under control?
Roland Yes.
Sidney Then I think for the moment you are out of danger.
Vanessa Oh isn't that marvellous. You were marvellous, Doctor. Wasn't he marvellous, Roland?
Roland (*wearily*) Yes, wasn't he.
Vanessa I think we should inform your wife though. I'll go and tell her.

Vanessa exits to the gardens

Roland You bastard! You could have strangled me.
Sidney Oh, I could have done willingly. You were going to tell that woman everything.
Roland All right, she's gone now. You can untie me.
Sidney Just stay there for the moment — while I decide what to do.
Roland There's nothing you *can* do.
Sidney Don't bank on it.
Roland Untie me, Sidney, or I'll yell out until somebody comes in.
Sidney Just be quiet.
Roland (*yelling*) Help.

Sidney starts to choke him again

Olivia enters from DL

Olivia Who was that? What's going on?

Olivia sees Sidney and reacts in a highly theatrical fashion

Oh my God, Sidney. You're alive. Oh, it can't be.

She staggers about clutching her heart. Sidney releases his grip

Roland Yes it is, he's alive.
Olivia Alive, alive.
Roland Yes, and he's trying to murder me.
Olivia Oh this is too much. It's like some dreadful macabre nightmare.
Sidney What is?
Olivia One son-in-law returns from the dead and tries to murder the other one.
Sidney I'm not trying to murder him.
Roland Yes he is. Help me, Olivia. If you hadn't come in I'd be done for. Look at me: I'm tied up. He's half-strangled me.
Olivia But why, Sidney? Why? What harm has poor Roland ever done to you?
Roland It's over the insurance money.
Olivia But you can't kill him for the insurance money. Unless you've insured him. Have you insured him?
Sidney No, Olivia. *Your* insurance money: he wants to give it all back.
Roland How about untying me?

There is a pause as Olivia undergoes a change of attitude

Olivia Just stay there for a moment. What do you mean give it all back?
Sidney He wants to tell them I'm alive and give it all back.
Olivia (*to Roland*) Oh, Roland dear. How could you? It would mean selling this place. All our hard work thrown away, and for what?
Roland I will not be a party to a fraud. I will not go to prison for five years. Now untie me.
Olivia Untie him, Sidney. He's a little overwrought, aren't you dear? I'm sure he'll be reasonable.
Sidney He'd better be.

Sidney begins to untie Roland with Olivia's help

Vanessa runs in from DL

Vanessa What incredible news.
Olivia What is?
Vanessa Your son-in-law is alive.
Olivia Oh him, yes. Yes, he's much better. We're untying him.
Vanessa No, not Roland, the first one, Sidney.
Olivia Sidney?
Vanessa Yes, he wasn't killed in that accident. It was somebody else. He's alive — and here.
Olivia Who told you this?
Vanessa Your daughter, Julia.

Julia in fairy queen outfit and broken wand enters DL

They all turn and look at her

Olivia I can't believe it.
Vanessa She said you wouldn't. Well, I must try and ring Henry before he leaves. He'll have to bring all the papers down. Won't be long.

Vanessa exits to the gardens

Roland You told her.
Julia I thought that's what you wanted.
Olivia Oh, you stupid girl.

Roland is rather pleased at this turn of events. Olivia and Sidney are thunderstruck, Julia unrepentant

Roland Don't get on to her. She did the right thing.
Julia At least it proves I love you.
Roland And I love you, darling.
Sidney Just hold on a minute. How much did you tell her? Did you tell her who I was?
Julia I just said my first husband was alive. I thought it would give you a chance to get away.
Roland There, that's all right then.
Olivia No it's not all right, it's not all right at all. I have no intention of giving that money back.
Roland Well we'll have to. It's a *fait accompli*, Olivia. Vanessa knows. Anyway I don't care what you do. Thanks to Julia, I'm in the clear.

Roland and Julia embrace

Sidney Oh no you're not. I'll say we planned it between us. I'll say it was a criminal conspiracy — and your idea.
Roland Oh you wouldn't.
Olivia Oh yes he would, dear.
Sidney Don't worry, Roland. I know my way around. I'll see you get a good job inside. How about the library?
Julia But Roland is innocent.
Sidney Well he'll be in good company. They all are.
Julia But you can't do this to him.
Sidney Oh can't I? You just watch me. All I have to do is get my story in first.

Sidney moves towards the gardens

(*Calling*) Vanessa. Mrs Harbinger.
Roland No wait, stop, stop ...
Julia Yes wait, Sidney, wait. We'll think of something.
Sidney Well you better be quick. She'll want to see this first husband back from the dead, and it's not going to be me.
Olivia No, but she'll want to see somebody, who else is there?
Roland How about McTavish?
Julia McTavish?
Roland Yes, he's in the office raving mad. She's never seen him.
Olivia You mean that dreadful chef who exposed himself.
Roland (*pointing to Sidney*) No, that was him.
Olivia Sidney?
Julia You?
Sidney Yes I admit I am the flasher from Madagascar.
Olivia Then who's in the office?
Roland The tailor's dummy in the waiter's uniform.
Olivia And the French doctor?
Roland That's him as well. Oh, and he was also the waiter and woodworm expert.
Olivia I'm sure I don't know how he does it. It's all too much for me. Julia dear, fetch me my smelling salts.

Julia exits DL

Olivia sinks on to the sofa

Vanessa enters from the gardens

Vanessa I'm afraid Henry has already left, so he'll be here in about forty minutes. (*To Olivia*) Are you all right, dear?

Olivia Oh, it's the shock. To think my dear, dead, son-in-law Sidney is alive.

Vanessa How long have you known?

Roland Oh, less than ten minutes.

Olivia In my case, five.

Sidney (*in a French accent*) In my case, even less.

Vanessa What happened? Did he just walk in?

Sidney No, he has been here all evening — but nobody recognize him.

Vanessa Then who did you think he was?

Roland Tell her, doctor.

Sidney McTavish.

Vanessa *McTavish.*

Sidney *Oui*, McTavish.

Vanessa But how could you possibly mistake ——

Roland Plastic surgery.

Sidney *Oui*. His whole face has been change. Nobody knew him.

Vanessa Could I possibly see him?

Roland Oh, I doubt it, he's a very sick man.

Vanessa Well you were very sick a short time ago.

Roland Well, that was Sidney. I mean the shock of finding he was McTavish.

Sidney Could I see you in the office.

Roland If you wish. Do excuse us.

Roland and Sidney go into the office

Vanessa sits down by Olivia on the sofa

Vanessa Any better?

Olivia Oh, a little. Poor Sidney, do you know what's wrong with him.

Vanessa They say he is hopelessly insane.

Olivia Oh, how dreadful.

Vanessa But he is alive, and from the Kindly Mutual's point of view, that's all that matters. We get back our money.

Olivia Yes, of course.

Vanessa Don't you want to see him?

Olivia I suppose I should.

The office door opens, and Roland hurries out and towards DL

What's wrong?

Roland An emergency. Sidney has collapsed. We're taking him to the treatment room.

Roland exits DL. *Sidney appears at the office door*

Vanessa Collapsed?
Sidney The news is not good. He has that deadly tropical fever.

Roland runs on with a medical trolley

Roland Here we are, Doctor.
Sidney Quick, hurry, hurry.

Roland ushers the trolley into the office and they close the door

Julia enters DL, *carrying a small bottle of gin*

Julia Here you are, Mother. Your smelling salts.
Olivia Oh there's a good fairy.

Olivia takes the bottle and half turns from Vanessa. She undoes the bottle and takes a swig. Vanessa cranes around and sees her

Vanessa Smelling salts?
Olivia Well, they're not actually for smelling.
Vanessa No, I gathered that. I was about to ask if I could have a sniff. Now could I have a snifter?
Olivia Well you may not like it.

Olivia reluctantly hands the bottle to Vanessa who removes the lid, and has a swig

Vanessa Oh, I don't dislike gin.
Olivia It's for medicinal purposes. I've had so many shocks.
Vanessa Yes, so have I. (*She takes another swig*) Shock after shock after shock. (*She takes another swig*) It began when your son-in law exposed himself. (*She takes another swig*) Then when I saw you in the plunge pool with the camel. (*She takes another swig*) Shock after shock.
Olivia I should leave a little for later. The shocks may not be over.
Julia How about me? What about the shocks I've had?

Olivia holds her hand out for the bottle and Vanessa somewhat reluctantly parts with it

Olivia Well you're young, dear and the young can cope. Besides, she hasn't left any.

Vanessa gives a slight hiccup. She is now very slightly drunk. Enough to numb her critical faculties

Roland comes out of the office

Roland (*gravely*) Bad news.

Olivia rises

Olivia Oh no, not more shocks. I can't stand it. Julia, get my other bottle of smelling salts.
Julia Yes, Mother.
Vanessa Oh, and tonic water and perhaps some ice?

Julia exits DL

Olivia (*severely*) This isn't a party, Mrs Harbinger. This is a family tragedy.
Vanessa Oh I know, dear — and I feel deeply for you. (*She rises with a little difficulty*) What's happened now?
Roland Sidney — is no more.

Olivia begins to slightly overact the role of a bereaved relative

Olivia Sidney? Dead?
Roland Yes.
Olivia Oh, I can hardly believe it. Just when he was restored to us, and he had so much to live for.
Vanessa Henry thought he'd get three years.

Olivia leans on Vanessa for support

Olivia Oh, how cruel fate can be — my favourite son-in-law.
Roland Thank you.
Vanessa What did he die from?
Roland Suicide.
Olivia Oh poor poor Sidney. I never even saw him.
Vanessa None of us did. I tried to see him — had I seen him I might have saved him.
Olivia So might I.
Vanessa Well perhaps we can see him now he's — no longer with us.
Roland I don't think that's wise.

Sidney comes out of the office

Sidney Well if they wish, they may see him. But stand well back.
Vanessa Why?
Sidney Because of the infection.

Vanessa and Olivia move upstage but Vanessa looks puzzled

Vanessa But Roland said it was suicide.
Sidney Oh, you told them that?
Roland Yes.
Sidney Yes, suicide following the infection. It was the infection which caused him to commit suicide.

Roland and Sidney go back into the office

Vanessa And poor Henry, what will he say? Dead, then alive, and now dead again.
Olivia Well if it upsets him, I shouldn't mention it.
Vanessa Oh I must.

Roland opens the office door wide and Sidney wheels out the trolley. On the trolley is a figure covered by a sheet with a chef's hat sticking out of one end, and a pair of boots sticking out of the other. (For reasons that will become obvious, this is not the actual dummy—whose head would be fixed on)

Vanessa moves towards the trolley

Sidney Stand back.
Roland Yes, for heaven's sake, stand back, Vanessa.
Vanessa Yes all right, but what *is* this infection?
Sidney The Madagascar Pding Pdong fever.
Vanessa Pding Pdong fever?
Roland Yes, Pding Pdong fever.
Sidney Caused by the deadly Pding Pdong Fly: one bite Pding — and then Pdong you have it. And from then on you are infectious — very, very infectious.
Roland Pding Pdong.
Olivia Could you remove his remains, Doctor — these awful tropical diseases make me nervous.
Sidney But of course. In Madagascar it is law that victims of Pding Pdong Fly have to be buried within ten minutes of their death.
Vanessa But that hardly gives time for a post mortem.
Sidney Believe me, madame. When they do a post mortem on a Pding Pdong case — they don't hang about.

Olivia Oh please please, just take him away.

Sidney is having trouble with the trolley

Sidney Of course, madame. Only I am having trouble with the trolley. The wheels have jam.
Vanessa Yes, I always have that trouble in supermarkets.

Roland holds the dummy's head between two straight hands as Sidney kicks the wheels straight at his end. Vanessa turns slightly away to cross upstage to exit

Well, I suppose I'd better go and inform the police.

At this point Sidney pulls the trolley off into the office

Roland is left holding the dummy's head. He is so shocked he doesn't notice

Roland The police?
Olivia Why the police?
Vanessa Because you have a sudden death.

Sidney runs on, takes the head off Roland, and runs off again

And that has to be reported to the police. I thought everyone knew that.
Roland It was fever.
Vanessa Followed by suicide. Well, I'd better waste no time. The position is complicated enough, insurance-wise.

Vanessa exits to the gardens

Roland's self-confidence now collapses. His nerves go

Roland The police. She's gone for the police.

Sidney runs out of the office

Sidney That's your fault, you idiot. Why did you say it was suicide?
Roland Because you didn't tell me what he died from. You're supposed to be the doctor.
Sidney Now don't panic. Let's just think.
Roland We're done for, Sidney. The police will come looking for a body and we haven't got one. They'll find the dummy ——

Olivia Then get rid of it.

Roland They'll search the place and they'll find it — and they'll know it's all lies. I don't want to go to prison.

Sidney Now pull yourself together.

Roland (*a broken man*) I don't want to go to prison. I don't care if I do work in the library, I don't want to go.

Olivia Roland, pull yourself together.

Roland makes an effort

Roland All right, I'm sorry. But we're done for.

Olivia No we're not, now where can we stick that dummy?

Roland You can stick it up the chimney for all I care.

Olivia Oh what a good idea.

Sidney You're right.

    Sidney runs into the office and comes back with the trolley. The proper dummy is now on it, fully dressed in the waiter's outfit

Come on give me a hand.

Roland reluctantly helps Sidney push the dummy up the chimney where it rests on a ledge out of sight. Roland, however, has hurt his back in the process

Roland Oh my back. I've twisted it.

Olivia Well go and lie down, dear.

    Julia enters DL *with a bottle*

Julia Here you are.

Roland (*taking the bottle*) Thanks.

Julia I had a job finding it.

Roland straightens up to take a swig from the bottle and screams

    What's up Roland?

Roland It's the tension — my back's gone. I can't straighten up.

Julia Oh no.

Roland And we're all going to prison. (*He straightens, swigs and screams*)

Olivia No we're not.

Roland Yes we are, and I won't even be able to work in the library. I'll never reach the upper shelves. (*He straightens, swigs and screams*)

Olivia Julia, take him to the treatment room. Run him a hot bath and put the heat lamp on him. (*Snatching the bottle from Roland*) And give me that.
Julia Come on, darling.

Julia helps the crippled Roland off. They exit DL

Sidney I hope the police don't start interrogating Roland. The first bit of pressure and he's going to crack.
Olivia Oh, you're right.
Sidney Can you lock that treatment room?
Olivia Yes.
Sidney Then wait until he's in the bath, take his clothes and lock them in.
Olivia What a good idea.

Sidney pushes the trolley and exits DL

I must say I miss having a crook in the family.

Olivia exits DL *after Sidney*

Hooper enters from the gardens. He takes another can of beer from his track suit top and opens it. Hooper is now quite drunk. He makes his way with some difficulty to the cupboard, stopping on the way for a swig of beer

He stands by the cupboard swaying for a while and then finally opens the door and goes inside the cupboard. He pulls the cupboard door shut

Vanessa and Sergeant Campbell enter from the gardens

Sgt Campbell So you think it may be a case of murder?
Vanessa Shhhhhhh. I didn't say that. I just said the death was highly suspicious.
Sgt Campbell Because of the insurance money?
Vanessa Exactly.
Sgt Campbell Well, where's this body?
Vanessa In here.

Vanessa and Sergeant Campbell go into the office and come out again

Well it was in there and now it's gone. Of course you must be used to that.
Sgt Campbell Used to what?
Vanessa Well, somebody reports a murder, and then when the police come, the body has vanished. Now you're not going to say I imagined it?

Sgt Campbell I'm not saying anything.
Vanessa Good, because it's around here somewhere. Just stay there and I'll go and find it.

Vanessa exits DL

Sergeant Campbell looks around and then hears a noise in the cupboard. She opens the door

Hooper stand there, swaying

Hooper Yes?
Sgt Campbell What are you doing in there?
Hooper Waiting for somebody.
Sgt Campbell I'm a woman police officer.
Hooper Well I'm not waiting for you.

Hooper shuts the cupboard door

Sergeant Campbell looks slightly baffled

Olivia enters DL

Olivia Oh, Sergeant. I was so sorry about your sandwiches — can I get the band some hard-boiled eggs?
Sgt Campbell Did you know there was a man in the cupboard?
Olivia No. But I'm not surprised. You see, we take a certain number of people who are — how can I put it — mentally unstable.
Sgt Campbell I see.
Olivia There is a new theory that much mental trouble is caused by a faulty diet. We have some astonishing results treating them with syrup of figs and raw cabbage.
Sgt Campbell Have you had any sudden deaths?
Olivia No. Not so far.
Sgt Campbell Well I've been told there's a dead body around here.
Olivia Well it's not one of ours.

Sidney enters DL *and then starts to exit again*

Ah, Doctor, this is our resident psychiatrist Doctor Louis.

Sidney takes Sergeant Campbell's hand in both of his and gazes into her eyes

Sidney *Enchanté, Mademoiselle l'Agent. Enchanté.*
Sgt Campbell Doctor, have you seen a body?
Sidney A body?
Olivia I think the sergeant has been talking to one of our special category
guests. (*She taps her head*)

Olivia exits DL

Sidney Ah, well of course. They are — are — how you call them in English?
(*He taps his head*)
Sgt Campbell Psychologically disturbed.
Sidney Yes, or as we say in French: bonkers.
Sgt Campbell (*opening the cupboard door*) Is he one?

Hooper is revealed, swaying and holding a can of beer

Sidney Oh, he is one. Yes.
Hooper Clear off.

Sidney spots the hamper on the floor

Sidney *Mon Dieu*, the wicker hamper.
Sgt Campbell Where?

*Sidney points to the wicker hamper in the cupboard. Hooper comes out of the
cupboard and looks down at the hamper as if he had never seen it before*

Sgt Campbell Is your name McTavish?
Hooper Certainly not. He's raving mad. They've got him locked up.
Sgt Campbell Did you take this hamper out of a minibus?
Hooper No, I found it in here.
Sgt Campbell Do you believe him, Doctor?
Hooper Doctor? He's not a doctor. He just says he's that so that he can
examine women. He's a Polish motor mechanic. All he came here for was
a woman. So if he wants to examine you, don't let him.

*Hooper takes another swig from the beer can, as Sergeant Campbell pulls the
wicker hamper out, and opens it. She looks inside*

Sgt Campbell Och. He's nearly eaten the lot.
Sidney So much for his special diet. Do you want to arrest him?
Sgt Campbell There's not much point if he's mentally unstable.
Hooper Who's unstable? I'm not unstable.

Hooper staggers and has to hold on to Sidney for support

Well perhaps I am slightly. But it's only because they starve me. Look at
me, I'm a human skeleton.
Sidney Go to your chalet and lie down, Mr Hooper.
Hooper I'm going. (*He weaves his way towards the gardens*) Going. (*He
stands by the exit*) Gone.

Hooper exits

Sidney Poor fellow. He is a sad case.

Vanessa enters DL

And here is another one.
Vanessa Ah, Doctor, what have you done with the body?
Sidney The body — which body? I have had so many.
Vanessa The one who had the Pding Pdong fever.
Sgt Campbell Had the what?
Vanessa A highly infectious fever from the Pding Pdong Fly. It bites you,
Pding, and five minutes later, Pdong, you're raving mad.
Sgt Campbell Have you been bitten by it?
Vanessa Good lord no. I've never been to Madagascar. Now where's this
body gone?
Sidney (*soothingly*) Please don't worry about it. Let's go and look for it, shall
we?
Vanessa And when we find it, we can show it to the sergeant.
Sgt Campbell (*drily*) Yes I'd like that.

Sidney and Vanessa exit DL

*Sergeant Campbell opens the wicker hamper and takes out a sandwich. She
sits on the sofa. She takes a bite out of her sandwich*

*Roland runs in from the gardens. He is wearing a dirty old raincoat, which
is now secured by safety pins and a piece of string tied around his waist.
He also wears a pair of fluffy pink lady's slippers*

*He sits down next to the Sergeant, who looks at him, with the sandwich frozen
in mid air*

Roland Are we alone?
Sgt Campbell Alone?

Roland Yes.

Sgt Campbell Well, I think so.

Roland Good, we haven't much time.

Sgt Campbell What for?

Roland I've got to get mine in first.

Sgt Campbell Get what in?

Roland My version of what happened. You see they had me locked up.

Sgt Campbell Oh, you were locked up.

Roland Yes, and they took all my clothes away. But I managed to get out of the window. I had to wear what I could. I had to borrow stuff off the wife. I mean I wouldn't normally wear these. (*He indicates the slippers*)

Sgt Campbell No, of course you wouldn't.

Roland Now where was I?

Sgt Campbell You got out of a window.

Roland Yes, I wanted to come and see you. I felt I *had* to come and see you.

Sgt Campbell Oh I see.

Roland Now what have they told you so far?

Sgt Campbell Well I've heard reports about a dead body.

Roland Ah now, let's start with that. I can tell you all you want to know about that.

Sgt Campbell You can?

Roland Yes. I was the one who bought it.

Sgt Campbell You bought it?

Roland In the auction. I didn't mean to buy it, it's not much use.

Sgt Campbell You bought a dead body in an auction?

Roland No no no. It was a dummy. It came with the camel.

Sgt Campbell You bought a camel as well?

Roland Yes. Now let's not waste any more time. Has he said anything about a criminal conspiracy?

Sgt Campbell Who, the camel?

Roland Sidney. Sidney Floyd Pucker. Now that is his real name. That's who he really is.

Sgt Campbell The camel?

Roland I'm sorry, Sergeant, but you seem to have an obsession about camels. I am talking about a man. The man who is supposed to be dead.

Sgt Campbell Oh, the dead body.

Roland Yes, now we're getting somewhere. Only of course he isn't dead. Because, you see, it wasn't him — and when he turned up here I gave him this old raincoat and he exposed himself.

Sgt Campbell Yes, that was reported earlier.

Roland Well he couldn't help it. He didn't mean to do it.

Sgt Campbell No?

Roland No, we mustn't blame him for that.

Sgt Campbell I understand the man who exposed himself was called McTavish.

Roland Yes, that's who I said it was. I mean I just pretended he was called McTavish.

Sgt Campbell And he had on that old raincoat you're wearing.

Roland He did yes. Only it's all respectable now. I've pinned it up — and tied it up, and it won't happen again.

Sgt Campbell Shall I tell you what I think?

Roland What?

Sgt Campbell I think it's you. I think you're McTavish.

Roland No, no, no. You've got it all wrong.

Sidney enters DL

(*Pointing to Sidney*) He's the one you want — not me.

Sidney (*with a French accent*) What are you doing out here, Roland?

Roland He's the one who exposed himself. He's McTavish, and he's wanted for fraud and Income Tax evasion — and antique faking. He's a master criminal. That's what he is, a master criminal, and he tried to strangle me — and he would have done if she hadn't come in.

Sergeant Campbell takes a notebook and pencil from her pocket

Sgt Campbell Now, I have to warn you that anything you say may be taken down and used in evidence.

Roland You hear that, Sidney? Anything you say is going to be taken down.

Sidney I think, Roland, she is talking to you.

Roland Me — why me?

Sergeant Campbell begins to write in her notebook

Sidney Because I think she is about to charge you.

Roland You've trapped me. You've caught me. I don't know how you've done it. My God, you're clever.

Sidney You've been a naughty boy, Roland. You have escaped from the treatment room, and somebody has broken the window.

Roland All right it was me. I did it. I admit it.

Sidney I'm afraid, Roland, you are in serious trouble.

Roland You've got to help me, Sidney.

Sidney Who is this Sidney? I don't know any Sidney. Now look at me: who am I?

Roland You're the doctor.

Sidney Doctor who?

Roland You're Doctor Who.
Sidney No I am Doctor Louis la Roullière.
Roland That's right. Yes, that's who you are. Yes.
Sidney You have been very uncooperative, Roland.
Roland (*babbling*) Yes I have. Oh I have yes. Yes I have. Yes.

*Sidney looks towards the fireplace and freezes for a moment. The dummy
slowly slides down the chimney and comes to rest in the fireplace. After a
moment, its trousers fall down. It is facing away from the audience. Roland
and the Sergeant do not see it*

  (*Continuing to ramble*) I haven't been well, you see ... not well ... I don't
  really know what I am doing ... I think I must be having a nervous
  breakdown.
Sidney Roland.
Roland Not well ... I'm not.
Sidney Roland, will you stop rambling and listen to me. I want you to get
  up and go over to the fireplace and do — what you have to. The sergeant
  will not look at you.

Roland gets up and sees the dummy

Roland You mean you want me to ...?
Sidney *Oui*. Don't look at him, Sergeant.
Sgt Campbell Do you mean he has to ...?
Sidney *Oui*. He know what he have to do.

*Roland crosses to the fireplace. He looks at the dummy and weighs up his
chances of convincing Sergeant Campbell*

Sgt Campbell In the *fireplace*?
Sidney It is better if people do not watch him while he is doing it.
Sgt Campbell I don't want to watch him, but isn't it a trifle unhygienic?
Sidney I'm afraid it is, yes.

Roland makes up his mind and points to the dummy

Roland (*shouting*) Have a look at this then. It's your last chance.
Sidney (*crying out*) Don't look.
Sgt Campbell I've no wish to.
Sidney Whatever you do, you must not look, it only encourages them.
Sgt Campbell Oh, I realize that.

Sidney I warn you, Roland. If the sergeant see that — she will arrest you here and now.
Sgt Campbell And we'll throw the book at you.
Sidney Now get on with it.

Roland's last bid has failed. Baffled and beaten he pushes the dummy back up the chimney

Sgt Campbell I know they can't help it, but why do you let him go in the fireplace?
Sidney I'm afraid it is the only place he will go.

Roland is having trouble pushing the dummy back up. Every time he pushes it up the chimney, it slides down again

Roland It's no good, I can't do it.
Sidney Well keep trying.

Roland finds he can only get the dummy out of sight by going up the chimney with it. So that his head and arms are out of sight

Sgt Campbell He seems to be a classic case of schizophrenia.
Sidney *Mais oui.* A classic case.
Sgt Campbell He has this alter ego called McTavish, on whom he blames his misdeeds.
Sidney *Mon Dieu*, you are right. But how do you come by this knowledge of psychiatry?
Sgt Campbell Oh, I'm a great reader. I also know you have to be firm with them — and that's why I've been scaring him.
Sidney And I think you've succeeded.
Sgt Campbell Has he finished yet?
Sidney Yes. He has gone up the chimney.
Sgt Campbell Done what?

The Sergeant turns round and looks, and then joins Sidney as they walk to the fireplace

Sidney He has these feelings of guilt and remorse, so he hides up the chimney.
Sgt Campbell Och, you can't help feeling sorry for him.
Sidney Oh, don't feel sorry for him. He is a pathological ingrate.
Sgt Campbell You mean he has to do it in the fireplace?
Sidney No, it means he is incapable of gratitude.

Sgt Campbell Oh of course, yes. It would do. I just wondered where he finally ...

She looks around the hearth. Sidney points to a large brass vase by the side of the hearth

Sidney We keep it there for that purpose.

Sgt Campbell Oh, that's no so bad then. It's a wee bit bizarre but it's not unhygienic. Well, I'll leave him in your hands, Doctor, and take this back to the band. (*She picks up the wicker hamper and moves to the gardens*)

Sidney And thank you, Sergeant, for your co-operation.

Sgt Campbell If you need any more help with him, call me.

Sidney Don't worry, I will.

Sergeant Campbell exits to the gardens

Sidney goes back to the fireplace

(*In his normal voice*) All right you can come down now.

Roland comes out of the fireplace

The dummy stays up the chimney

Roland You evil swine, Sidney.

Sidney Don't abuse me, Roland. A moment ago, you were begging me to help save your skin.

Olivia enters from the gardens

Olivia Roland, what are you doing dressed like that?

Roland I escaped.

Julia enters DL. *She is now wearing a white overall coat*

Julia Yes, and I helped him. How dare you lock us up.

Olivia It was for your own good. Has he spoken to the police?

Sidney Oh he has. He's told them everything.

Olivia Everything?

Roland Yes, and now they think I'm the flasher.

Julia If anyone's interested I finally found the key.

Sidney runs over to her, as she takes the key from her pocket

Sidney God bless you, my dear — and I only hope you'll be as happy with
him as you were with me. Bye-bye, Olivia, bye-bye, everyone. Madagascar, here I come.

Sidney exits DL

Olivia Well now, it rather looks ——

Vanessa enters from the gardens

— as if we shall have to keep the insurance money.
Vanessa Not so fast, Olivia. there's something very suspicious going on —
and I know Henry will want to investigate when he gets here.
Roland Investigate what? I promise you everything is absolutely above
board.
Vanessa So you say. But I saw Julia's first husband lying dead on a trolley.
Now where is he?

Sidney runs on DL

Sidney (*in a French accent*) Eh, *voilà*! I have found him.

*Sidney runs off and appears immediately wheeling the trolley, on which
lies a body (Hooper), completely covered in a white sheet*

There he is, madame, Julia's first husband: Sidney Floyd Pucker.

The body under the sheet slowly sits upright, still covered by the sheet

Vanessa Oh he's alive. Oh, Henry will be pleased. He's not dead.

The sheet falls from around the body revealing Hooper, who is still drunk

Julia He's not my husband.
Vanessa What?
Roland No of course he isn't.
Vanessa But why did everyone say he was? And why did you say he was
dead?
Olivia Well he was dead *drunk*.
Hooper Who's drunk? I'm not drunk — all I've had is a sip of sparkling spa
water. (*He lies flat on the trolley*).
Roland Yes of course, that's it. The spa water. I'm afraid Vanessa we have
kept something from you.

Vanessa What?

Roland Owing to a substance in that spa water, we have all been hallucinating.

Vanessa Hallucinating?

Roland Yes, we've had it analysed. The spa water has been passing through a stratum of some powerful hallucinogen such as — Mexican Peyote mushrooms — or L.S.D.

Sidney But of course. That was why I thought this man was dead.

Roland And why Olivia thought she was being drowned by a camel.

Vanessa But I saw her.

Olivia Oh you couldn't have done. I imagined it.

Sidney Did you drink some of the spa water?

Vanessa Only a drop.

Roland Obviously you had a drop too much.

The dummy slides slowly down the fireplace, its trousers round its ankles. Vanessa sees it and points

Vanessa Look, look — McTavish.

Roland Where?

Vanessa In the fireplace, with his head up the chimney.

Olivia But there's nobody there.

Vanessa Nobody there?

Sidney Nobody.

Roland Nobody.

Julia Nobody.

Vanessa Oh my head is going round. I didn't like to mention it, but why is Roland wearing that dirty old raincoat?

Roland I'm sorry but this is my best white coat.

Vanessa And are you naked underneath it?

Julia No of course he isn't. Show them, Roland.

Vanessa Yes, show me.

Roland Very well.

Roland slowly unpins the safety pin and throws it down like a male stripper. Then he undoes the string and casts that aside, and then, with a big gesture, he throws open the raincoat. Underneath he is wearing the fairy queen dress. Vanessa staggers back in horror

Vanessa Oh you're right. You're right. I *am* hallucinating. Oh promise me one thing.

Olivia And what's that?

Vanessa Promise you won't tell Henry.

Roland Oh we promise.

Roland
Olivia } (*together*) We promise!
Julia

C<small>URTAIN</small>

FURNITURE AND PROPERTY LIST

ACT I

On stage: Reception desk. *On it*: guest register. *Above it*: key-board with keys
Wall fountain-type water dispenser with tap. *Above it*: "Cliffbank
    Magna Waters, drink freely" sign
Paper cup container with cups
Chest of drawers. *In drawers*: odds and ends
Three-seater sofa
Wooden Windsor armchair
Screen. *Behind it*: life-size dummy on hospital trolley with menu-card
    as script
Fireplace. *On hearth*: brass vase
Cupboard. *In it*: various odds and ends

Off stage: Suitcase (**Vanessa**)
Plastic shopping bag containing tin of chocolate wafers (**Olivia**)
Old raincoat (**Roland**)
Waiter's trousers (**Roland**)
Walking stick with spike (**Olivia**)
Tape recorder (**Vanessa**)

Personal: **Sidney**: sunglasses, two passports, large red handkerchief, two cigars
Roland: two pencils
Julia: small torch

ACT II

On stage: As before

Off stage: Wicker picnic hamper containing two cans of beer, sandwiches in
    plastic wrapping, bag of doughnuts (**Hooper**)
Plastic bag containing fairy queen costume (**Olivia**)
Fairy queen dress (**Julia**)
Tape recorder (**Vanessa**)
Clothes line with assorted laundry attached, including pair of lady's
    tights (**Vanessa**)
Hospital trolley (**Roland**)
Small bottle of gin (**Julia**)

Hospital trolley with dummy's head and bolster under sheet to represent dummy's body (**Sidney**)
Hospital trolley with complete dummy in waiter's uniform (**Sidney**)
Bottle of gin (**Julia**)

Personal: **Sgt Campbell**: police notebook and pencil
Julia: broken wand
Hooper: can of beer
Julia: key

LIGHTING PLOT

Property fittings required: nil
Interior. The same scene throughout

ACT I

To open: Full, general lighting with sunny evening effect from gardens

No cues

ACT II

To open: Full, general lighting with dusk effect from gardens

No cues

EFFECTS PLOT

ACT I

Cue 1   **Olivia**: "The very acme of trash food."   (Page 5)
         Telephone

Cue 2   **Sidney** is heard blowing his nose loudly off stage   (Page 6)
         Gurgling noises from the fountain

Cue 3   **Vanessa** goes to water dispenser and squirts some water   (Page 19)
         Gurgling and hooting noises from the fountain

Cue 4   **Olivia**: "... and offers them jobs."   (Page 27)
         Loud crash

Cue 5   **Roland**: "... I'm a chocoholic."   (Page 27)
         Loud crash

Cue 6   **Roland** shuts cupboard door   (Page 34)
         Ship's siren noise from fountain

ACT II

Cue 7   To open Act   (Page 37)
         *Optional: very faint jazz music heard intermittently in the
            background from the garden*

Cue 8   **Sidney** closes the office door   (Page 40)
         Sound of crashing

Cue 9   **Sergeant Campbell** takes a drink from the water dispenser (Page 42)
         Subdued noise from fountain

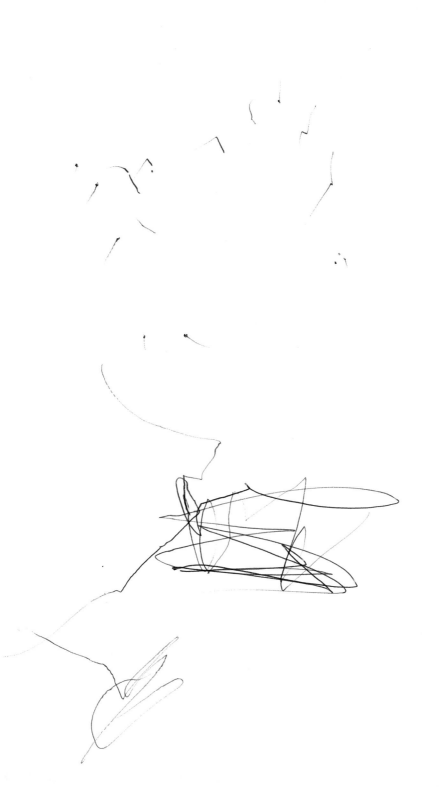